Synkrētic

The Journal of Indo-Pacific
Philosophy, Literature & Cultures

2023 / № 4

Synkrētic
The Journal of Indo-Pacific Philosophy, Literature & Cultures

ISSN 2653-4029

Editor: Daryl Morini
Deputy Editor: Christian Romuss

www.synkretic.com

General enquiries: enquiries@synkretic.com

Correspondence should be addressed to

> The Editor, Synkrētic Journal
> c/o Irukandji Media Pty Ltd
> Unit 9 204 Alice St
> Brisbane City Qld 4000
> AUSTRALIA

Synkrētic acknowledges the traditional custodians of the lands of Brisbane on which we work, the Turrbal and Jagera peoples.

Published in Australia by Irukandji Press, Brisbane.
Irukandji Press is a trade name of Irukandji Media Pty Ltd.

ISBN 978-0-6454980-2-8

Layout and editorial matter: © Irukandji Media Pty Ltd, 2023

Essays, responses, stories and notes: © retained by respective authors or their estates and (re)printed here with permission OR source is in the public domain.

The moral rights of the authors have been asserted.

All rights reserved. No part of this publication may be reproduced, stored in a retrieval system, or transmitted in any form by any means without the prior permission in writing of the Editor of Synkrētic.

Cover design and typesetting: Arthur Arek

Contributors

Maulana Muhammad Ali · Georges Baudoux
David Gegeo · Akshay Gupta
Mysore Hiriyanna · Philipp Mainländer · Theresa Meki
Daryl Morini · Aaron Ortner · Noel S. Pariñas
Krishna Pathak · Christian Romuss

Acknowledgments

Synkrētic №4 (Apr. 2023) was a collaborative enterprise involving 12 past and current writers and oral history sources from 8 countries across the region.

Contributors to this issue were based in Australia (3), Germany (1), India (2), New Caledonia (1), Pakistan (1), the Philippines (1), Solomon Islands (1), and the United States (2).

Synkrētic warmly thanks all rights holders from around the world whose support made this issue possible.

Contents

On the varieties of Indian thought   1

ESSAYS

David Gegeo
Revitalising Indigenous good governance in Solomon Islands   7

Theresa Meki
On Kruksie's awareness of the unseen   30

Mysore Hiriyanna
Fording the troubled ocean of *saṃsāra*   37

Philipp Mainländer
The philosophy of redemption   51
    TRANSLATED BY *Christian Romuss*

Maulana Muhammad Ali
The religion of Islam   73

RESPONSE   *What is Indian philosophy?*

Aaron Ortner
The art of living in harmony   87

Akshay Gupta
The problem of evil in Hindu thought   95

Krishna Pathak
The Eastern wisdom of ancient India   100

STORIES

Georges Baudoux
The first white men   111
    TRANSLATED BY *Daryl Morini*

NOTES

Noel S. Pariñas
On comparative philosophy   129

EDITORIAL

On the varieties of Indian thought

Issue four of *Synkrētic* focusses on Indian philosophy, a tradition which Mysore Hiriyanna notes begins almost two millennia before Christ and spans over thirty centuries.

Hiriyanna emphasises the essential differences between the diverse traditions that split off into orthodox and heterodox doctrines across the history of Indian philosophy. These have included the Vedānta, Buddhism, Jainism, and other schools which have been ascendant at various times.

It is a complex picture that resists easy generalisation, one made more complicated, according to Hiriyanna, by the fact that we know comparatively little of the lives of the great Indian philosophers, unlike the historical sources that exist in the Western canon, such as Diogenes Laërtius' *Lives of the Philosophers* and Plato's works for the life of Socrates.

But Hiriyanna does attempt to sketch some common threads across these traditions, including that in India philosophy was not sundered from religion, aimed beyond logic and ethics, was seen as a way of life and not just as a way of thought, aimed at *mokṣa* or liberation, and cultivated an ascetic ideal of discipline to attain it.

In his interview, Aaron Ortner notes the historical diffusion of Indian ideas to Ancient Greek thinkers like Heraclitus, in whose system he sees a Greek equivalent of the Indian concepts of *mokṣa* and *samsara*. He also fascinatingly finds similarities between the *Iliad* and the *Mahābhārata* and the *Odyssey* and the *Ramayana*.

Akshay Gupta's analysis of the problem of evil in the *Bhāgavata Purāṇa*, one of the most important Hindu sacred texts, offers another incidental but tantalising connection between Indian and Western thought, which also has a tradition of theodicies—justifications of God's existence in the face of evil—including in the works of Thomas Aquinas.

In a wide-ranging interview, Krishna Pathak offers a thought-provoking case for why Indian and Hindu thought should be taught at Western universities, particularly the founders of various philosophical schools of the classical period, and proposes a list of subjects that merit attention.

Pivoting to the Pacific, David Gegeo passionately argues for revitalising Indigenous good governance in Solomon Islands, contrasting this Western concept with the conflict resolution practices and epistemology of the Kwara'ae people.

In a moving essay, Theresa Meki reflects on the passing of her grandfather Kruksie, who was from the Eastern Highlands Province in Papua New Guinea. The story of Kruksie's life and death is surrounded by the mysterious phenomena of the unseen, such as the appearance of the *papa graun* or spirits of the land.

With a similar focus on spirits and also in Melanesia, the two translations of Georges Baudoux which appear in this issue narrate the stories of the Indigenous Kanak people of New Caledonia from the perspective of a white French settler novelist. Both stories, the comical 'That old Tchiao' (1919) and the more macabre 'A horror story' (1939), are published in English for the first time in this issue.

Also appearing for the first time is an extract from Christian Romuss' forthcoming translation of the German philosopher Philipp Mainländer's *The Philosophy of Redemption*. 'God has died and His death was the life of the world,' Mainländer argues in his magnum opus, the first volume of which will be published later this year.

Still on the topic of God, Maulana Muhammad Ali's *The Religion of Islam* (1936) argues that Islam is the true religion for the whole of humanity, that it is the religion of peace, and that it is the religion of all the prophets of God, including those of the Torah. Islam 'is an all-inclusive religion which contains within itself all religions which went before it,' he strikingly writes.

In the final piece of the issue, Noel S. Pariñas reflects on comparative philosophy. 'Claiming a comparison between Eastern and Western philosophies is problematic because philosophy is funda-

Synkrētic

mentally Western,' he argues. This is an important point for *Synkrētic* itself as a comparative journal of Indo-Pacific philosophy.

Daryl Morini

ESSAYS

Revitalising Indigenous good governance in Solomon Islands

*David Gegeo**

As an integral part of the rising tide of political decolonisation and feminist counter-hegemonic movement in the 1960s, the 1970s and 1980s ushered in *epistemic decolonisation*. Although it may come under different terminologies and interpretations, the overarching theme or target of epistemic decolonisation is the decolonisation of the social construction and use of knowledge in the global South as well as among minority groups and women in the global North. In fact, it is duly acknowledged that some of the movement's most audacious and articulate front-liners are feminist academics and professionals of diverse ethnicities in the global North.[1]

While as a counter-hegemonic movement epistemic decolonisation can be described as achieving global recognition in the 1970s and 1980s, as a narrative or social discourse it has historically been symbiotic with political decolonisation. Both are often applied with equal audacity to sterilise metro-centric androcentrism from its historical dominance over the social construction of knowledge. In fact, political decolonisation is the physical performance or activation of epistemic decolonisation writ large.

Epistemic decolonisation is informed by a host of questions such as: Who should have the right to create knowledge and for whom? Is there knowledge which transcends all geophysical and socio-on-

---

* David Welchman Gegeo is Associate Professor and Director, Office of Research and Postgraduate Affairs, Solomon Islands National University. He holds a PhD from the University of Canterbury. He lives in Honiara, Solomon Islands.

tological boundaries as to be rightfully called universal knowledge? Who has the expertise to construct such knowledge and where is it constructed? Whose epistemology, methodology, pedagogy, ontology, and hermeneutics inform the construction of such knowledge? As knowledge is generally equated with power, the underlying message of such questions is obviously the bigger question of who overall has the right or power to dictate over other groups in the social construction and use of knowledge.[2]

The long-felt need for epistemic decolonisation is made clear by the fact that, despite strong resistance, at times vitriolic attacks, by mainstream political, academic, and religious bodies, especially in the global North,[3] it has never lost momentum and instead, empowered by those vitriolic attacks, has unabatedly been gaining vitality and exactitude in voice and vision globally. This resilience can be gauged in numerous ways such as the burgeoning literature which includes alternative research paradigms anchored in epistemologies, methodologies, ontologies and hermeneutics of the global South,[4] the inclusion of minority group subjects in school curricula,[5] and a greater recognition of the contributions of women and minority groups to the well-being of the global community through education, research, advocacy for peace and racial harmony, healthcare, and other lines of work.

Other issues of concern in epistemic decolonisation involve the challenging question of how relevant or legitimate indigenous knowledge systems are in today's rapidly globalising world. The concern is particularly critical in formerly and still colonised societies where the impact of colonisation was, and is, of such a magnitude that indigenous knowledge systems are treated with contempt as unsalvageable relics of humanity's primordial past best left to rust to make space for the global proliferation of metro-centric ways of knowing, doing, and being. The meta-message of *epistemicide* or the killing of indigenous peoples' knowledge systems, in this case Pacific Island peoples' indigenous knowledge and languages, is clear.[6]

In sharp contrast, when advocates of epistemic decolonisation address the legitimacy of indigenous knowledge systems and languages, it is in the true spirit of community social activism, empowerment, and cultural re-vitalisation. It is stated with apprehension, however, that today menacing epistemicide is for the most part practised or committed by Pacific Island communities themselves as an indelible legacy of colonisation or unconscious devaluation of cultural knowledge. The menace is evidenced by *endophobia*, the syndrome of expressed dislike for one's own race or ethnicity in favour of *xenophilia*, the love of or desire for strangers and their cultural practices as evidenced by the adoption and practice *en masse* of Christianity and English or French in place of indigenous religions and languages by most Pacific Island communities, a process that began from the time of first European contact and continues today.

Epistemic and linguistic change is inevitable and experienced in every human society. However, for all practical purposes, menacing epistemicide and menacing linguicide in Solomon Islands should be closely monitored as so much has already been lost due to colonisation. There is no approach more strategically effective to doing so than Solomon Islands communities themselves re-embracing *endophilia*, the love for, respect for, and keeping of one's indigenous cultures and knowledge systems alive and functional through everyday active social practice.

Community re-embracing of endophilia must be the first fundamental step to controlling menacing epistemicide and menacing linguicide because no remedial policy or program, however scientifically sound, can succeed without it. And the reason is that the human agency required to drive it successfully to fruition is deeply engrained in endophilia itself. It should be noted though that, while deemed most effective, the re-embracing of endophilia by communities cannot be expected to take full effect overnight because it is a dynamic process of social and psychological re-building or transformation requiring major attitudinal change. The critical point to underscore is that, to be fully achieved, the re-embracing of endophilia must be set into motion with confidence and with trust fully invested in its inherent efficacy for desired positive change.

Scope and focus

Embracing the ethos of epistemic decolonisation, this paper argues for the reassertion of indigenous epistemology, ontology, and axiology in the interest of re-vitalising Kwara'ae indigenous governance and conflict resolution practices. Of particular attention is the issue that, as new cultural practices are introduced from abroad through globalisation, they get contextualised by taking on new cultural characteristics as they are acted upon by groups in Kwara'ae and Solomon Islands more generally. As the new cultural practices go through greater acculturation, they become doubly problematic relative to when they were first introduced.

The scenario is exemplified by 'rural-urban drift', in which young women and men leave their rural communities to find employment in town to earn cash to send back home to meet family obligations. However, once in town, free from the watchful eyes of culture and families, they do as they please, indulging, for example, in alcoholism, nightlife, and other behaviours typical of urban life. Ultimately, it is ineffective to address the new societal developments by metrocentric knowledge alone and indigenous knowledge must therefore be strategically incorporated into solution-seeking efforts.

Methodology

This essay was prompted by work on peace, reconciliation, and good governance which I have been involved in with various civil society organisations and government ministries in Solomon Islands. Data for the paper came from this work as well as an extensive review of the literature on Solomon Islands ethnic tensions which occurred from 1999 to 2003[7], and ongoing research on the role of indigenous epistemology, ontology, and hermeneutics in decolonisation, development, and the impact of globalisation on Solomon Islands and other Pacific Island societies. The paper employs a critical framework in examining issues, however it is not itself a criticism of what should or might have been done by the Solomon Islands government and communities to prevent the last national ethnic tensions and other societal crises such as urban riots from occurring.

In critically examining issues pertinent to the re-vitalisation of Kwara'ae indigenous governance and conflict resolution practices, I use specific examples from Kwara'ae and, where relevant, other Solomon Islands cultural groups. I now turn to a discussion of governance and conflict resolution practices in Kwara'ae, starting with a brief literature review of good governance more generally followed by good governance reviewed from a Kwara'ae perspective.

Governance and society: a brief literature review

In the growing need for alternative strategies to effectively curb the escalating rate of conflicts and violence in Solomon Islands over land ownership and chronic corruption in government leadership, an epistemological approach which has been promoted since the 1980s is *governance*. The concept *governance* was first coined by the World Bank and subsequently exported pre-packaged to countries around the world, especially in the global South, as the epistemology deemed most effective for minimising socio-economic and socio-political turmoil.

As if to suggest that governance was not effective enough, the World Bank later coined the sub-genre *good governance* as a more effective form of governance for promoting socio-economic and socio-political equilibrium in societies.[8] The World Bank defines the term as follows:

> Good governance includes the creation, protection, and enforcement of property rights, without which the scope for market transactions is limited. It includes the provision of regulatory regime that works with the market to promote competition. And it includes the provision of sound macroeconomic policies that create a stable environment for market activity. Good governance also means the absence of corruption, which can subvert the goals of policy and undermine the legitimacy of public institutions that support markets.[9]

As can be seen from this definition, good governance as the long-awaited panacea for subverting deleterious conditions in countries of the global South is firmly anchored in not one but several epistemological and methodological principles or domains, of which the most commonly referenced are *accountability, participation, predictability*, and *transparency*. There are inherent challenges in investing unconditional trust in the frame of good governance. For one, defined even on the basis of a clear understanding of the constituent principles, good governance still eludes a deeper understanding, especially among the general public, of its importance in society. Simai poignantly addresses the issue thus:

> the concept of the increasingly fashionable category of "governance" has yet to achieve a universally accepted definition… in certain languages governance simply means "the management of household". Culture, together with other key factors (geographic and historical conditions, for example), is one of the most enduring variables conditioning and influencing the forms and content of governance.[10]

For another, there is a tendency among academics and other professionals to give greater emphasis to economic issues only. This not only blurs or narrows the epistemological scope of good governance but also makes economics seem the only cause of corruption and conflicts, hence explaining the retardation of national development in Pacific Islands and other societies of the global South. The tendency is exacerbated by good governance being top-down, deeply embedded in the epistemologies, methodologies, and ontologies of the global North. This is despite repeated strong arguments to incorporate in good governance bodies of knowledge drawn from the epistemologies, methodologies, axiologies, and ontologies of Pacific Islands and other societies of the global South.[11]

The issue of defining and understanding good governance would perhaps be less cumbersome if it were simply semantic, but it is ontological as well. Ontologically, the challenge stems from the underlying assumptions that the constituent principles of good governance always function maximally well together in every situation when in practice they do not. What actually happens is that the sphere of influence or extent of the effectiveness of each and all of the principles is determined by human agency which in turn, as Simai has argued,[12] is influenced by cultural, gender, economic, and environmental factors. And speaking more specifically about how good governance is hard to achieve due to the lack of accountability at the intergovernmental and organisational levels, Keohane states that:

> the entities conventionally held accountable on a transnational level ... are major intergovernmental organizations concerned with economic globalization: the European Union, World Bank, International Monetary Fund, and the World Trade Organization. These organizations are major targets of demands for accountability. They certainly have deficiencies in accountability. They do not meet democratic standards of accountability as applied in the best-functioning democracies in our era.[13]

And so, when good governance is achieved it is because human agency maximises the effectiveness of the constituent principles. Thus, for example, if conflict resolution practices in a given society are robust and every person who causes conflict is held *accountable*, then the domain or sphere of effectiveness of *accountability* will expand or intensify. If the same scenario holds for *participation*, *predictability*, and *transparency*, then good governance is realised and society is in a state of socio-political and socio-economic equilibrium. Conflicts and resultant violence are greatly minimised.

However, if human agency counteracts the domains or spheres of effectiveness of the constituent principles, *i.e.*, people are not held accountable for causing conflicts and so conflicts and concomitant violence occur more frequently, then bad governance becomes normalised social practice. The normalisation of behaviours or social practices ordinarily considered antithetical to good governance practices is a red flag to be avoided at all costs, as it means in the final analysis that society has either entered or is on the verge of socio-ontological disequilibrium.

Good governance and conflict resolution: A Kwara'ae indigenous perspective

In Kwara'ae indigenous epistemology and social ontology, good governance and conflict resolution practices are mutually inclusive.

Indigenous good governance in Solomon Islands

Conflicts arise because society lacks good governance such as resources being mismanaged—the lack of *transparency*—especially at the national and provincial levels, resulting in social inequality, which provokes the disadvantaged segment of society to take to the streets in angry protest. Conflicts therefore have to be resolved to restore good governance. An alternative reading suggests that the literature on good governance and conflict resolution in some important respects pays inadequate attention to the myriad cultural and environmental factors which can influence the constituent principles and hence the status of good governance and conflict in Kwara'ae. Take, for example, the principle of *participation* which basically argues that, through open dialogue and mutual engagement in events, disputing parties will come to understand one another better and hence settle their differences in a manner conducive to lasting resolution.

However, empirical evidence from Kwara'ae research suggests otherwise. In many instances disputing parties may civilly engage in face-to-face open dialogue and activities yet refuse resolution if, in their hearts and understanding, they believe the causes of conflict to lie elsewhere or issues have been 'resolved' in a manner not respectful of their cultural principles or protocols.

Moreover, the emphasis on the 'lack of understanding' explanation inherent in the principle of *participation* seems excessive. For example, in Kwara'ae culture many chronically unresolved conflicts, some going back in origin to the last century, are between tribes which have known each other inside out through sharing land boundaries and resources, mutual engagement in community development projects, church affiliation, family obligations, *etc*. Besides, many are closely related through marriage. Yet the tenacity with which some of these tribes have clung to the issues causing conflicts between them defies rational thought, whether in Kwara'ae or other Solomon Islands cultures.

For example, one of the tribes most notorious for causing conflicts in Kwara'ae constantly brags about being the first indigenous people in the area to be Christianised, and on the basis of this prides itself on being the most 'modernised' and hence the power-house of peace, social justice, and economic development in their communities. The tribe had indeed been involved in different church-related community development projects, none of which had panned out in any meaningful way due, ironically, to the lack of good governance in their management. As for its claim to being an exemplary promoter of good governance, community residents have been contemptuous, arguing rather that it is a notorious chronic instigator of land disputes which have seen it driven from one falsely-claimed land to another. Today the tribe lives precariously on borrowed land, courtesy of the land-owners, apprehensive about where to relocate next should it be asked to leave.

The scenario is not unique to this tribe but is true of many tribes in Kwara'ae and Solomon Islands. It dates back to the 1800s when, in order for Christian missionaries to have easy access to indigenous tribal groups for purposes of religious conversion, large mission villages were built on the coast upon mutual agreement between indigenous tribal land owners and European missionaries. This culminated in an exodus of genealogically unrelated tribes from the mountains to live together in the mission villages. Conflicts arising from clashes between tribes due to different cultural practices was a regular occurrence, which the missionaries had myopically neglected to give serious thought to. Some tribes, over time, tired of the constant conflicts, returned to the mountains, much to the dismay of the missionaries, and successfully reclaimed ownership of their original tribal land. Other tribes were not so fortunate. The scenario has since the 1960s been made worse by globalisation, physically manifested through large-scale logging and other deleterious money-making activities.[14]

From the cases described, it is clear that the 'lack of understanding' explanation inherent in the principle of *participation* seems to mean one thing in metro-centric good governance and conflict resolution discourse and quite another in that of the Kwara'ae. In metro-centric conflict resolution discourse the explanation seems to be that, in order to reach a level of understanding necessary for conflict resolution, members of the quarrelling parties must first develop good rapport among themselves.

In contrast, in Kwara'ae indigenous conflict resolution practices it is important but not absolutely necessary that good rapport be established between rivalling parties as the first step toward conflict resolution. The more important understanding is directed at the causes of conflict and appropriate cultural mechanisms with which to resolve it. In fact, promoting good rapport between rivalling groups is seen as potentially compromising as it can cause a *softening of hearts*, which can make a land dispute resolution based not on facts but emotion.

I would like now to discuss more specifically indigenous governance in Kwara'ae. I reiterate that the objective of this paper is not to debunk the World Bank's version of governance but rather to show that the Kwara'ae, like most cultural groups in Solomon Islands, have been practising governance in varied configurations since time immemorial. Accordingly, when metro-centric governance, or any other metro-centric body of knowledge for that matter, is introduced into Kwara'ae, the objective ideally should be to bilaterally identify points of structural and epistemic confluence between the two distinct paradigms of governance. In this way, a new bi-epistemological paradigm of governance is co-constructed within which local communities promote socio-ontological equilibrium in society.

The argument, admittedly, is not new, in fact is commonplace, yet it is confounding how metro-centric governance, or any other metro-centric bodies of knowledge for that matter, always seem to hold sway *vis-à-vis* indigenous governance when it comes to designing and implementing policies and programs. In short, metro-centric knowledge still dominates, whether for good or ill, reflecting the syndrome of *xenophilia* discussed earlier, whereby the majority of Solomon Islanders show greater preference for metro-centric knowledge and social practices than those of Solomon Islands indigenous cultures. It should be clarified that the argument for the re-embracing of endophilia is not to completely debunk xenophilia, which at this stage in Solomon Islands' development is not possible. The point rather is to strike a balance or identify a point of epistemic and structural confluence where relevant introduced and indigenous bodies of knowledge are applied with equal strength in the building of a society where, despite great cultural and linguistic diversity, all Solomon Islanders can live together in peace and harmony.

Gwaumauri'anga as indigenous good governance

Before the importation of the World Bank's brand of good governance in Solomon Islands in the 1980s to de-escalate rising violence, Kwara'ae, like most Solomon Islands cultural groups, had long developed and been practising their own indigenous governance. This truism is substantiated in myriad ways such as by the indigenous cultural practices of '*adofiku'anga* (inter-dependence) and *tua barangwaiasina'anga* (egalitarianism), which involve Kwara'ae communities always looking out for each other's safety and well-being. Specifically, the Kwara'ae word for good governance or an approximate socio-ontological state of existence is *gwaumauri'anga*.[15]

Gwaumauri'anga is the noun form of *gwaumauri*, an intransitive verb consisting of two morphemes combined, *gwau* which means 'head' and *mauri* which means 'live, alive, or to be living', while *'anga* is the noun form meaning 'the process or state of'. *Tua* is sometimes added before *gwauamauri'anga* to emphasise staying, being, or living at the highest peak of life. Similarly, *tua'a,* which means 'family', 'household', or 'kin group' is sometimes uttered before *gwaumauri* to mean a family or kin group which has achieved the ideal state of *gwaumauri'anga*. Accordingly, a woman, man, or child from such a family or kin group is described as *kini gwaumauri*, *ngwae gwaumauri*, and *ngela gwaumauri* respectively. A *tua'a gwaumari* is generally referred to as *tua'a 'a'ana*, a senior family. And a *gwaumauri* tribe is referred to as *fu'ingwae lalifu*, a firmly rooted tribe.

Gwaumauri'anga, which takes generations to achieve, is defined or characterised by the ownership of an abundance of natural resources such as land replete with virgin forests and food sources of all kinds, flowing streams, and rivers, rolling hills, *etc.*, which makes a tribe self-sufficient and relatively independent. Children and adults are healthy and happy and have a sense of self-assuredness and purpose. Families are loving, respectful of other people and willing to help other families and tribes in times of need. They are respected for possessing the human qualities of being peace-loving, humility, intellectual vitality, oratorical skills, leadership skills, stability, high ethical standards, artistic skills, *etc.*

As a human social construct or achievement, *gwaumauri'anga* is, of course, not etched in stone and so is susceptible to change. In light especially of the incessant rupture of Kwara'ae indigenous sociocultural ontology by the unrelenting forces of globalisation, several Kwara'ae tribes have expressed concern over the sustainability and longevity of their *gwaumauri'anga*. For example, community fission and displacement due to conflicts between indigenous land owners and government-backed transnational logging and mining projects going back to the 1930s have had tremendous adverse impacts on the *gwaumauir'anga* of many Kwara'ae indigenous communities. Colonisation, of course, had also dealt a series of lethal blows to *gwaumauri'anga* in Kwara'ae by indiscriminately destroying indigenous theocracy, leadership, spirituality, and the overall sense of cultural integrity, being, and belonging.[16]

Growing individualism, intrinsic to global materialism, is a culturally egregious new challenge which is also exerting tremendous adverse impact on *gwaumauri'anga* in Kwara'ae society by undermining such important cultural values as *'adofiku'anga* (interdependence), *fangale'a'anga* (sharing), *alafe'anga* (love), *kwaisare'e'anga* (giving without expectation of a return), *etc*. Practised in myriad ways, the phenomenon is most conspicuously enacted in the way certain opportunist tribal members, usually young university-educated males knowingly acting afoul of tribal consent, singlehandedly sign behind closed doors lucrative business deals with logging, mining, fishing and/or resource-grabbing transnational business conglomerates. The menace to *gwaumauri'anga* is intensified by a sharp decline in *fa'amanata'anga*, a vitally important indigenous cultural tradition of teaching or counselling through which the ten key cultural values of Kwara'ae society are passed on to children and young adults.

To be perpetuated for future Kwara'ae generations, *gwaumauri'anga* requires the same community collectivist work ethic and unconditional, deep commitment to Kwara'ae socio-cultural ontology, which had established it in the first place. The positive news, however, is that a tribe cannot actually lose its *gwaumauri'anga* in total once established. Rather, it may go through periods of high and low intensity in its *gwaumauri'anga* such as when, for one reason or another, it is not making any cultural accomplishment or contribution to society and so is publicly viewed as *nene* (quiet, inactive), or *anoano* (hauntingly silent).

Naturally, whispers of curiosity and sometimes malicious ridicule circulate in the communities as to why the once *gwaumauri* tribe seems to be retreating into *anoano'anga* (chilling haunting silence). Suddenly, after some time has passed it emerges with renewed energy and vitality from its *anoano'anga* by way of making a dramatic cultural accomplishment such as throwing a lavish feast to commemorate some important cultural event, which simultaneously also rekindles tribal and community ties in the area and so effectively *ta'efaolo ana* (resurrects or restores) its *gwaumauri'anga*.

Such a public demonstration of resilience to adversity is characteristic of a *gwaumauri* tribe which readily lends credence to the truism that once established, a tribe cannot lose its *gwaumauri'anga* in total, as mentioned. One of the reasons for this is tribal ownership of abundant natural resources such as land, which literally form the bedrock of tribal *gwaumauri'anga*. It should also be mentioned that, rapid social change notwithstanding, periods of low intensity are rarely experienced in *gwaumauri'anga*.

Epistemic constituents of gwaumauri'anga

In discussions of good governance as conceived by the World Bank, academics and other professionals tend to emphasise the four key principles mentioned earlier—namely *accountability, participation, predictability*, and *transparency*—as foundational. Of the four principles, *accountability* and *transparency* tend to be given the greatest weight as being the most indispensable for realising good governance. The other two principles are usually mentioned in passing.

By contrast, *gwaumauri'anga* is firmly anchored in ten or more key cultural principles, namely: *alafe'anga* (kin love, kindness); *aroaro'anga* (peace, peacefulness); *babato'o'anga* (stability, calmness); *enoeno'anga* (humility); *fangale'a'anga* (sharing); *kwaigwale'e'anga* (welcoming, comforting, hospitality); *kwaima'anga* (love, kindness); *kwaisare'e'anga* (giving without expectation of a return); *saesaele'a'anga* (happiness, gladness); and *mamana'anga* (truth, honesty, sacred power).[17] The ten key cultural principles are always evoked with equal weight in the adjudication of community disputes over land and other issues and discussions of Kwara'ae socio-cultural ontology more generally, especially in *fa'amanata'anga*, as discussed shortly.

I will now discuss in detail some of the key epistemic constituents of *gwaumauri'anga* to give an idea of the nature of each and how in maximally functioning well together as a system they keep *gwaumauri'anga* and hence Kwara'ae society on a socio-ontological equilibrium. In the interest of time and space I will be discussing only five of the epistemic constituents.

Alafe'anga: The arm that binds in Kwara'ae society

Of all the key cultural values identified by Watson-Gegeo and Gegeo, *alafe'anga* reigns supreme as the all-embracing value of Kwara'ae indigenous socio-cultural ontology. *Alafe'nga* can be so described because it is the cultural principle through which all the cultural values constituting Kwara'ae indigenous socio-cultural ontology are publicly expressed in everyday social behaviour. *Alafe'anga*, in other words, is the all-embracing cultural value which interconnects and permeates all the cultural values and through which the practice of all Kwara'ae key cultural values are mirrored.

Alafe'anga is composed of the verb *alafe-* which means 'to love' or 'to be loving' in the sense of kin love, and the noun-form *-anga* which means 'the act or process of loving'. It is clear that without *alafe'anga* no Kwara'ae cultural value can be cognitively constructed, much less physically practised such as *gwaumauri'anga*. The all-embracing value of *alafe'anga* is shown by the fact that it is the cultural value which is always strongly emphasised in all forms of social discourse in Kwara'ae society, from *fa'amanata'anga*, the epistemology of formal cultural socialisation, to *kwalabasa'anga,* the epistemology of everyday social interaction.[18]

Alafe can be used to describe the behaviour of an individual, a family, village, tribe, or community. A person who is described as *alafe* or having *alafe'anga* is also described as *ali'afu*, being whole or complete, in the sense of having mastery of and living according to the key cultural principles of Kwara'ae indigenous socio-cultural ontology. Similarly, a child who shows a proclivity for *alafe'anga* is touted as being on the path to achieving *ali'afu'anga*.

Alafe'anga's indispensable role is apparent in that all the key cultural values perform their respective roles in upholding *gwaumauri'anga* at its command. For example, *aroaro'anga* (peace or tranquillity) strongly reflects *alafe'anga*, as does *amani'anga* (truth, honesty, vitality). In the final analysis, *alafe'anga* can be described as the principal social force which connects all the key cultural values and informs them of their respective roles in ensuring *gwaumauri'anga*, and therefore Kwara'ae society as a whole, stays in balance.

Ali'afu'anga: The holism of Kwara'ae society

Ali'afu'anga, one of the key cultural principles of Kwara'ae indigenous socio-cultural ontology, is the noun form of the verb *ali'afu* which, loosely translated into English, means 'to be complete' as in a circle or cycle or process. The word consists of two morphemes, *ali-* which means twirl or spin around as of a rope around a tree, and -*'afu* which means 'complete'. It is the view, or sense, of completion or completeness in a cycle or process where every part dovetails so perfectly that no flaw or deformity can be detected. Thus, for example, when all the parts required to complete a task or process have been assembled and the task is completed to the ultimate degree of expert performance such that no flaw can be detected, the task is described as *ali'fu*. The slightest deformity renders the work flawed, *'iri 'ali'afu*, not complete and so unacceptable. *Ali'afu* can also be applied to the acquisition of knowledge or skills in a subject such as history, genealogy, culture, *etc.* such as an individual who possesses an expansive body of knowledge about something as to be highly respected as a tribal elder or leader and is called *gwaunga'i*, head-hood or head-ness.

Epistemologically, *ali'afu'anga* can perhaps be aptly defined by the concepts of *epistemic holism* or *epistemic ambidexterity* when used in reference to people, in that an *ali'afu* person is someone who is well-rounded in commanding both theoretical and practical knowledge in some field of study or expertise in Kwara'ae indigenous culture. Ultimately, *ali'afu'anga* conveys the notion of a cycle, process, need, or goal having reached or been achieved at the highest peak of success.

Kwalongwae'anga: Endless love in Kwara'ae society

The root word of the noun *kwalongwae'anga* is *kwalongwae*, which is two morphemes combined: *kwalo* meaning string or twine, and *ngwae* meaning human or person; *'anga* is the noun form and means the process or state of. As a principle in Kwara'ae indigenous socio-cultural ontology, *kwalongwae'anga* means the welcoming of people or humans. However, more fundamentally, it connotes the idea of boundless love that welcomes endlessly no matter how long the queue of people is.

Kwalongwae'anga's indispensable role in *gwaumauri'anga* is obvious in that a *gwaumauri* tribe or individual is one which habitually shows endless and unconditional love for other people regardless of the circumstances. Accordingly, a typical scenario of a *kwalongwae* family is one in which a mother meets at the village entrance and leads a long queue of visiting relatives to her house, engaging them in warm, welcoming, casual conversation. The husband in the meantime is waiting in the house to receive the visitors, showing them where to sit, *etc.* while food is being prepared. If he is away in the gardens, the mother will send one of her daughters or sons to collect him. The guests and members of the host family will be addressing one another not by their real names but by kin terms such as aunt, mother, son, sister, father, uncle, cousins, *etc.* to evoke and reaffirm the sacrosanctity of genealogy. At the end of the visit, the couple and their family members and relatives will see their guests off at the village entrance the same way they welcomed them on arrival.

Ala'anga: The social discourse of Kwara'ae society

The ten key cultural values that constitute the essence of *tua gwaumauri'anga* are taught through an indigenous cultural tradition or epistemology called *fa'amanata'anga* .[19] So fundamental to *tua gwaumauri'anga* in Kwara'ae society is *fa'amanata'anga* that every Kwara'ae child as young as two or three years is introduced to it by his or her parents or older siblings. *Fa'amanata'anga* is nestled in and conducted through another cultural tradition called *ala'anga* (talk, meeting, or council).

Held usually in the village *gwaurau* (meeting house), either in the morning, afternoon, or evening, formal *ala'anga* is a public event in which different kinds of conflicts are heard, from simple conflicts such as two young children fighting to more serious and complicated ones such as land disputes. *Ala'anga* to settle simple matters are usually presided over by the village chief or chiefs. Evidence is presented and adjudicated according to the principles of Kwara'ae *falafala* (culture). For example, after everybody has gathered in the *gwaurau*, the presiding chief would open the *ala'anga* by making the pronouncement that there has been some *firu'a* (entanglement) in the village and he has called for an *ala'anga* to *fa'asaga* (straighten out) and *rokea* (disentangle) it.

Based on the evidence presented to him and the other village residents, the chief renders his verdict. He would then close his remarks by emphasising that *gwaumauri'anga* is the tower of force or strength at whose feet they dwell, or the *bibi* (foundation) of Kwara'ae society. *Gwaumauri'anga* emerges from the ten key cultural principles practised in totality. After the conflict has been resolved, the village chief or elder would then call upon a village elder or elders to start the *fa'amanata'anga* in light of the conflict. Occasionally, a village chief might invite another chief or chiefs, usually ones more senior than him, from other villages to adjudicate a conflict if he cannot do it himself.

Fa'amanata'anga: Kwara'ae epistemology of counselling and conflict resolution

Ala'anga embraces another cultural event for conflict resolution and the teaching of cultural values and social practices called *fa'amanata'anga*, translated in English to roughly mean 'shape the mind', 'cause to think', or 'counselling'.[20] An elaborate discussion of how *fa'amanata'anga* is done is provided by Watson-Gegeo and Gegeo (2014).[21] *Fa'amanata'anaga* is cross-generational in that members of the younger and older generations are involved with the *fa'amanata* (counsellors), who are chiefs or elders. There are two kinds of *fa'amanata'anga*: private, *fono*, and public, *'ifi*. Public *fa'amanata'anga* usually involves a large gathering of people such as a whole village, an extended kin group, or even a tribe. It is, however, not open to just anybody. For example, any non-kin visitor to the village noticing a *fa'amanata'anga* in session will leave immediately out of respect for its sacrosanctity. The most noticeable sign of a *fa'amanata'anga* in session is silence in the village. Children are kept at home and told not to make any noise. Adults converse in a low and whispering manner. It is usually held in the *gwaurau*, the village meeting house, either in the late afternoon or evening.

Public *fa'amanata'anga* may be deemed necessary for two reasons. First, an event has occurred such as violation of a cultural taboo or land dispute which has caused social instability in a village or community and needs to be resolved to restore socio-ontological equilibrium. After the dispute has been resolved, *fa'amanata'anga* then follows. Second, it is an occasion on which tribal chiefs and other elders may simply wish to bring their people together to touch base on village or community matters after some time has passed. The topics covered usually are the epistemic constituents of *gwaumauri'anga*. However, the presiding chief may also request from the audience other important topics for *fa'amanata'anga*, such as community women feeling that their important traditional role as productive members of Kwara'ae society is constantly being eroded by the forces of globalisation. The presiding chief will ask the proponent of a topic to briefly describe it, after which he and other village elders then start *fa'amanata'anga*.

Private *fa'amanta'anga*, in contrast, is an exclusive family affair in which parents counsel their children behind closed doors usually in the evening after dinner. The parents take turns in *fa'amanata'anga* with the topics ranging from simple everyday etiquettes to the more serious epistemic constituents of *gwaumauri'anga*. However, a session could also address more specifically the misbehaviour of one of the children in the family such as petty theft or negligence to carry out an assigned family task. The misbehaving child is interrogated as to the reasons for the misbehaviour. The parents emphasise how the misbehaviour is having a negative impact on both their reputation and that of the family. Private *fa'amanata'anga* occurs more frequently than public *fa'amanata'anga*.

Fa'amanata'anga stands on precarious ground

Today *fa'amanata'anga*, disturbingly, stands on precarious ground, the result of new developments, the most authoritarian of which, ironically, is the proliferation of metro-centric-style schools and education in rural communities. The proliferation has in effect rendered obsolete—'their time is finished'—women and men most renowned and respected for their depth and breadth of indigenous knowledge and *fa'amanata'anga* skills in Kwara'ae society. The situation is compounded by the current generation of Kwara'ae parents looking to metro-centric-trained school teachers and schools as the structural and epistemic transformation of traditional elders and the community respectively, and so expect them to be solely responsible for the *fa'amanata'anga* of their children.

No attitude, of course, could be more myopic. An effective and talented *fa'amanata'anga* teacher is not university-educated but rather firmly steeped in Kwara'ae *falafala* (culture or socio-cultural ontology) by virtue of having been socialised through *fa'amanata'anga* since early childhood and practising it in adulthood. *Fa'amanata'anga*'s menacing demise is exacerbated by the proliferation in rural and urban communities of store-bought videos, mobile phones, and other technical gadgetry on which children and young adults watch foreign movies, and play games and music for hours instead of attending *fa'amanta'anga* sessions when held.

The neglect or refusal of *fa'amanata'anga* by the present generation of Kwara'ae women and men is a regrettable case of poor judgment, which entails losing more than just a supposedly archaic cultural tradition. More fundamentally and seriously, the neglect entails being deprived of access to the epistemic conduit or vehicle through which the very essence or core substance of Kwara'ae indigenous socio-cultural ontology is passed onto future generations of Kwara'ae, namely: epistemology, ontology, hermeneutics, methodology, axiology, critical thinking skills, the proper use of Kwara'ae language, oratory, spirituality, cultural etiquette, genealogical knowledge, *etc*.

The possession of these bodies of knowledge amounts to *ali'afu'anga,* the socio-ontological state of human development and intellectual maturity which defines and towards which all Kwara'ae women and men strive in life. In the final analysis, *fa'amanata'anga* is in effect the cultural epistemology, methodology, and axiology through which a Kwara'ae person is able to construct the ultimate desired identity of *tua 'o'olo'anga,* living in righteousness, cognisant of the difference between right and wrong. Furthermore, while *gwaumauri'anga* is anchored in land, it is *fa'amanata'anga* which nurtures it by virtue of instilling in generations of Kwara'ae cultural values and behaviours indispensable for upholding and perpetuating it, as evidenced by the epistemic constituent principles discussed.

Conclusion

On the heels of political decolonisation in the 1960s followed in the 1970s and 1980s *epistemic decolonisation* or the decolonisation of knowledge construction and use in both the global North and global South. Most audacious and articulate in the movement were and are women of diverse ethnicities and disciplinary persuasions who targeted what they saw as the historically overbearing and androcentric nature or taste of knowledge construction and use globally. That is, knowledge construction has historically been the prerogative of white middle-class males and therefore predominantly reflects their truth and belief. The experience and epistemological capability of women and minority groups have historically been either belittled or simply denied legitimacy in knowledge construction and use.

Meanwhile, in the global South, epistemic decolonisation was and still is a step behind the global North, in that the primary target was and is not so much the de-masculinisation of the epistemic contents of the social construction of knowledge *per se*, but rather the prevention or control of the wholesale importation of culturally irrelevant and often outmoded metro-centric knowledge and accompanying technology. The practice continues unabated despite repeated strong arguments by researchers and educators in both the global North and global South to contextualise metro-centric knowledge so as to make it more culturally and epistemically relevant and to therefore have a greater success rate or applicability in the activities, such as national development, for which it was and is imported into the global South.

Good governance as imported from the World Bank by the Solomon Islands government in the 1980s as the long-awaited panacea for national catastrophe fell short of its intended purpose because it was culturally and epistemically irrelevant, and deployed in a context of chronic mismanagement in the Solomon Islands. Kwara'ae *gwaumauri'anga* is an example of Solomon Islands indigenous good governance which, because of epistemic and cultural relevance, has mitigating potential for de-escalating chronic conflicts and concomitant violence nationally. It is confounding that the great wealth of indigenous knowledge embedded in *gwaumauri'anga* and other Solomon Islands indigenous governance, having such indefatigable capacity to produce lasting resolutions to national conflicts, is hardly tapped into by national planners and decision-makers.

Notes

1. Linda Tuhiwai Smith, *Decolonizing Methodologies: Research and Indigenous Peoples* (Dunedin: University of Otago Press, 2005); Kristie Dotson, 'Tracking Epistemic Violence, Tracking Practices of Silencing', in *Hypatia*, Vol. 26, No. 2 (Spring 2011), 236-257; Linda Alcoff and E. Porter (eds.), *Feminist Epistemologies* (New York: Routledge, 1993); Lorraine Code, *What Can She Know?* (Ithaca, NY: Cornell University Press, 1991); Sandra Harding, *Whose Science? Whose Knowledge?* (Ithaca, NY: Cornell University Press, 1991).
2. Nora Berenstain, Kristie Dotson, Julieta Paredes, Elena Ruíz, and Noenoe K. Silva, 'Epistemic oppression, resistance, and resurgence', in *Contemporary Political Theory*, Vol. 21, No. 2 (2022): 283-314; Gaile Pohlhaus, 'Relational Knowledge and Epistemic Injustice: Toward a Theory of Wilful Hermeneutic Ignorance', in *Hypatia*, Vol. 27, No. 4 (Fall 2012): 715-735; Sabelo J. Ndlovu-Gatsheni, 'The Dynamics of Epistemological Decolonization in the 21st Century: Towards Epistemic Freedom', in *Strategic Review for South Africa*, Vol. 14, No. 1 (2020): 16-45.
3. Cassandra L. Pinnick, Noretta Koertge, and Robert F. Almeder (ed.), *Scrutinizing Feminist Epistemology* (London, UK: Rutgers University Press, 2003).
4. N. K. Denzin, Y. Lincoln, and L. Tuhiwai Smith (eds.), *A Handbook of Critical and Indigenous Methodologies* (Los Angeles, CA: SAGE, 2008); David Welchman Gegeo and Karen A. Watson-Gegeo, '"How We Know": Kwara'ae Rural Villagers Doing Indigenous Epistemology', in *The Contemporary Pacific*, Vol. 13, Issue 1 (2001), 55-88; Jane Duran, *Toward a Feminist Epistemology* (London: Rowman and Littlefield, 1995).
5. bell hooks, *Yearning: Race, Gender and Cultural Politics* (New York: Routledge, 2014).
6. Boaventura de Sousa Santos, *Epistemologies of the South: Justice Against Epistemecide* (London: Paradigm Publishers, 2014); Ndlovu-Gatsheni, 'The Dynamics of Epistemological Decolonization in the 21st Century'.
7. Clive Moore, *Happy Isles in Crisis: the historical causes for a falling state in Solomon Islands, 1998-2004* (Canberra: Asia Pacific Press, 2005).
8. Graham Hassall, 'Good Governance, Human Rights and Conflict Resolution', in John Henderson and Greg Watson (eds), *Securing a Peaceful Pacific* (Christchurch: University of Canterbury Press, 2005).
9. World Bank, quoted in Paul Cammack, 'The Governance of Global Capitalism: A New Materialist Perspective', in Rorden Wilkinson (ed.), *The Global Governance Reader* (New York: Routledge, 2005), 163.
10. Mihaly Simai, *The Future of Global Governance* (Washington, D.C: United States Institute of Peace Press, 2005), xxii-xxiii.

11 John Henderson and Greg Watson (eds), *Securing a Peaceful Pacific* (Christchurch: University of Canterbury Press, 2005).
12 Simai, *The Future of Global Governance*.
13 Robert O. Keohane, 'Global Governance and Democratic Accountability', in Rorden Wilkinson (ed), *The Global Reader* (New York: Routledge, 2005), 128.
14 David Welchman Gegeo, 'Indigenous Knowledge and Empowerment: Rural Development Examined from Within', in *The Contemporary Pacific*, Vol. 10, Issue 2 (1998): 289-316; David Welchman Gegeo, 'Tribes in Agony: Land, Development and Politics in Solomon Islands', in *Cultural Survival Quarterly*, Vol. 15, No. 2 (1991): 53-56.
15 Gegeo, 'Indigenous Knowledge and Empowerment'; Gegeo and Watson-Gegeo, '"How We Know": Kwara'ae Rural Villagers Doing Indigenous Epistemology'.
16 Gegeo and Watson-Gegeo, '"How We Know": Kwara'ae Rural Villagers Doing Indigenous Epistemology'; David Welchman Gegeo and Karen A. Watson-Gegeo, 'Whose Knowledge: Epistemological Collision in Solomon Islands Community Development', in *The Contemporary Pacific*, Vol. 14, Issue 2 (2002): 337-409.
17 Gegeo and Watson-Gegeo, 'Whose Knowledge: Epistemological Collision in Solomon Islands Community Development'; Gegeo and Watson-Gegeo, '"How We Know": Kwara'ae Rural Villagers Doing Indigenous Epistemology'.
18 Karen A. Watson-Gegeo and David Welchman Gegeo, 'Heavy Words and Important Silences: Kwara'ae Children learning the indigenous epistemology of willingness and rank', in *Pacific Studies*, Vol. 37, No. 3 (December 2014): 172-201; Gegeo and Watson-Gegeo, 'Whose Knowledge: Epistemological Collision in Solomon Islands Community Development'.
19 Watson-Gegeo and Gegeo, 'Heavy Words and Important Silences: Kwara'ae Children learning the indigenous epistemology of willingness and rank'.
20 Karen A. Watson-Gegeo and David Welchman Gegeo, 'Social Identity, Church Affiliation and Language Change in Kwara'ae (Solomon Islands)', *Papers in Pragmatics*, Vol. 4, No. 1-2 (1990): 150-182.
21 Watson-Gegeo and Gegeo, 'Heavy Words and Important Silences: Kwara'ae Children learning the indigenous epistemology of willingness and rank'.

On Kruksie's awareness of the unseen

*Theresa Meki**

On the 19th of May 2022, Kruksie passed away. Kruksie was my maternal grandfather from Marikente or Marix village in the Henganofi district of the Eastern Highlands Province in Papua New Guinea. His real name is Maigao Tembero. Maigao and Tembero are both names from the Kote language of Finschafen in the neighbouring Morobe Province—most likely given to the family by Lutheran missionaries from Finschafen. His parents were Tembero and Atao. Maigao, also known as Kruksie, was the first of eight siblings. After him came Togo, Frankie, Aputi, Steven, Esther, Pius, and Junis. Kruksie married Neinkenaso or Nunake and together they had seven kids, Dennis (who passed away as an infant), Kekas (my mother), Mao, Patrick, Amon, Ruben, and little Kekas (my auntie is named after my mother).

I was in Canberra when he passed away and could not afford to travel home for his *haus krai*[1] and his funeral. However, I did send some monetary contribution for the building of his tomb. Surprisingly, his death did not affect me as much as I thought it would. Maybe because Kruksie was very old—he had lived to a ripe old age and with all his faculties deteriorating he needed to rest. To him, death was a welcome relief from pain. The thing about death is that

---

* Theresa Meki is a Pacific Research Fellow with the Department of Pacific Affairs, Australian National University. She holds a PhD from ANU. She lives in Canberra, Australia.

Synkrētic

it forces you to think about life. The brevity of it, the struggle, the possibilities, memories, and the mystery behind it.

I thought about Kruksie—his life, the type of person he was, his skillset, traditional knowledge, and period of his life. I concluded that perhaps he was the last of his kind or type of person. I am not sure of the appropriate terminology, but he was someone who was in tune with both the material and the spiritual realm. I'll use the rest of this essay to explain what I mean and, in the process, memorialise my Kruksie.

Kruksie must have been born around 1938 or 1939. My uncle Amon told me that when Kruksie was a little boy he saw lots of planes fly over, which must have been the Second World War. My mother was born in 1966 and her older brother Dennis would be about two or three years older than her. Back in those days, men still lived in the men's house and as a method of family planning were instructed to not reside with their wives until their baby was walking about, around two years of age. Hence, most siblings were between two to three years apart. Suppose Uncle Dennis was born in 1963, Kruksie would have then been around twenty-five years old. But as a young man, before Kruksie became a father, he worked briefly in one of the gold dredges in the Bulolo Valley.[2] He returned to Henganofi where his parents and uncles had an arranged marriage prepared for him.

Nunake, the betrothed (my grandmother), was taken from her village of Haiafaga as a child and lived with Kruksie's parents until she reached puberty. Sometime after she started menstruating the marriage ceremony was organised, and she and Kruksie became husband and wife. I was sad when Nunake first told me about this because I don't think she got to experience carefree fun as a child or as a teenager. Still a child, her life was decided and planned for her. Sad as it was, that was how life was like back then for girls.

But perhaps the wisdom of the elders proved correct with this arrangement because Kruksie and Nunake were quite compatible. Both did not have a lazy bone and were very industrious until old age prevented them from working. After his brief work experience at Bulolo, Kruksie worked as an office assistant at the Henganofi station government building where he was given a small flat. Unlike his two brothers Steven and Togo, who went to work and live out their adult lives in major towns, Kruksie as the first born of the Tembero family stayed back in Marikente village. Together with the help of Nunake, he established himself as a leader due to his generosity in organising feasts and distributing food, particularly pig meat.

Purpose of this piece

Kruksie's life spanned the duration of a PNG society in transition from colonialism to independence, from traditional to modern and post-modern life. His Tok Pisin was very good, so I heard a lot of interesting anecdotes from him, but as he aged his Kafe vernacular became his primary language and as a non-Kafe speaker I missed out on a lot of good conversations.

One story that I still remember clearly was when he talked about what life was like before the missionaries came. For the highlands, that would have been before the 1930s because the Lutheran missionaries came into the Eastern Highlands after the 1930s. Before the missionaries brought the gospel into the area, spirits interacted freely with them. Kruksie told me of this one time when the spirits came and took him, lifted him in the air, and flew him to another area close to the village cemetery and dropped him there. At other times, the spirits would hang around the river and whenever someone went to wash or do laundry they would poke fun at them by playfully splashing water or causing them to trip over. It sounded like these spirits were good-natured and didn't mean any harm to the locals. However, they did take issue with strangers.

From his stories, it seemed like the spiritual, unseen world was interspersed with the living. These spirits are sometimes referred to as 'nature' or *'papa graun'*.[3] Kruksie said that when the missionaries came with the gospel and started to build churches, these *papa graun* went away to hide in the big bush. But there are times, if they are not happy with the land or the way things are being done, when they will communicate through either dreams, visions, or some other type of metaphysical incident to express their dismay. But there are certain people who have the privilege of receiving communication from or having an awareness of the intentions of these *papa graun*. From Kruksie's experiences, I believe he was one of those few people who had this cross-dimensional awareness.

Vignette 1: Awareness of the unseen

Between 1983 and 1984, Kekas (my mum) brought my dad Jonah to her village. They were dating at the time. They decided to go help in the family coffee garden, a small plantation. It was coffee season and a lot of hands were needed to collect coffee cherries. Prior to Jonah entering the garden, Kruksie went ahead and spoke to the bush. He said, 'your children are here to see the place so take care of them while they are here.' He had to introduce my dad to the bush because that was his first time visiting and Kruksie did not want the *papa graun* to regard him as a stranger. After working for a few hours, it started to get chilly, and my dad decided to take a smoke break. So, he sat down near a small fire and quickly dozed off into a much-needed nap. In a dreamlike vision he saw short, chubby, and skinny people surrounding him with bows and arrows; it looked like they were ready to pounce on him. Then suddenly, a giant-looking man came from behind and scared off those little pigmy people. My dad, now frightened, told my mum about the dream. When they told Kruksie, he just said, 'Oh, that giant of a man was my grandfather looking out for you. He was a fierce warrior.'

Vignette 2: Knotted stomach

A few weeks prior to his death in May 2022, Kruksie's stomach had turned into knots and he couldn't pass stool for days. He was in terrible pain and could barely walk. He called and cried to my mum explaining his pain—something was not right. Mum quickly called her two brothers Ruben and Mao, who lived in the village, and chastised them. She instructed them to quickly go buy a carton of meat, make a *mumu*,⁴ and feed people. For whom exactly and for what occasion, she did not specify. She said, 'Just do it'.

Apparently, a couple of days prior to Kruksie's stomach situation, Ruben had arranged for a bulldozer to come flatten a little mountain next to the Okuk highway near our village. It seems that the unseen landowners were not happy with that action—that's why they knotted Kruksie's stomach. Anyway, my uncles quickly purchased a carton of sheep meat, bought vegetables from the market, made a *mumu* and called people in the village to come eat. In addition to the *mumu*, the uncles also slaughtered a pig, collected its blood into a dish and, using *tanget* leaves,⁵ sprinkled the blood onto the surrounding area where the landscape was changed. That very night, Kruksie finally did a number two. The message was, 'before you make any drastic changes to the landscape you need to appease the unseen landowners or *papa graun*.'

When my mother called and reported this to me, I recalled that more than a decade ago, probably around 2008 or 2009, when the PNG Liquified Natural Gas (LNG) project was under way and construction was starting in the Southern Highlands Province, there were so many stories coming out of that province about giant snakes retreating into the bigger bush, being upset and angry. These giant snakes, or '*traipla moran*' as the locals called them, were omens or manifestations of *papa graun*. I found all of this very intriguing.

Moreover, there are only certain people in the village, usually older men or women who are privileged to get these types of dreams or communications from the *papa graun* or the unseen. For us, Kruksie was one of them. He might have even been our last. The type of person who is aware of what 'nature' wants and whom nature chooses to communicate with. I don't think this type of privilege, wisdom, or responsibility can be passed down to the next generation. It certainly wasn't passed down to my uncles, as they were quite ignorant of the implications of their action with bulldozing that huge chunk of land. At least my mother had the insight to interpret Kruksie's cry accurately. Instead of rushing him to the hospital—which is what I would have done—she called for a *mumu* to appease the *papa graun*.

Synkrētic

Vignette 3: Controlling the car

Kruksie had that connection with the land right until his death. The next and final vignette is a bit surreal, but it happened. That's the main reason I must write it down, because eventually I will forget, and my mum and uncles will forget and then it will be like it never happened.

On the night that Kruksie passed away, which was around 2am on 19 May 2022, he died peacefully. He did not struggle. Only his son Ruben was near him when he passed. Ruben called my mum and his brother Patrick in Goroka town, but they didn't hear the phone. They were all fast asleep. He rang until 3am when, finally, his niece Anko answered her phone and relayed the message to everyone in town. By 3:30am they left Goroka and drove to Henganofi, arriving around 4:30am. The Goroka family travelled to Henganofi with two vehicles. An outback Totoya LandCruiser and a Toyota ten-seater.

Upon their arrival, they carefully wrapped Kruksie's body in a blanket and carried him into the ten-seater. Ruben and my mum sat behind with Kruksie, and Patrick got in the driver's seat to drive. Other relatives piled into the outback LandCruiser. As they were about to leave, Patrick started the car, but the engine suddenly died. Patrick got out of the car and lifted the bonnet to check the battery. It was fine. He tried to start the car again. Still nothing. Patrick, being a mechanic, checked everything else with the car and it all seemed fine, but why would it not start?

At this point, all Kruksie's children started thinking hard. What did they do to cause this? Mao, usually quiet, spoke up. He said, 'we rang for a long time and you guys in town did not pick up the phone quickly. Also, all this time when Kruksie was getting really old and feeble you guys hardly ever visited him.' While Mao generalised this accusation, the siblings knew that he was referring to their brother Patrick. Of Kruksie's children, Mao, Ruben, and little Kekas lived with their families in Henganofi, so they were always nearby to look after him. My mum, despite living in town, visited him almost every other weekend and had built him a house. His other son Amon lived eight hours away, worked in a Chinese company and had no time to visit. But Patrick, unfortunately, did not pay much attention to Kruksie—he was preoccupied with his mechanic work and family. It was like Kruksie was saying, 'when I was alive, you never came and took me out driving and now you want to drive me away?'

Patrick came around into the back seat of the car. He gently held Kruksie's cold feet, and he apologised. He said, 'I'm sorry that I was too busy making money and taking care of my own family that I did not come visit you regularly when you were alive. Please have peace so that we can go.' Patrick returned to the driver's seat, started the engine, and the car roared back to life. It was strange but made sense to everyone there. Kruksie's spirit was not happy—that's why the car didn't start—and once that was acknowledged he allowed them to take him to the funeral home.

Notes

1. *Haus krai*: A site for mourning, a temporary shelter usually built quickly to accommodate friends and neighbours who will visit the bereaved during their time of mourning. *Haus krai* also refers to the period from when the deceased resides in the funeral home until the day of burial.
2. Hank Nelson, *Taim bilong masta: The Australian involvement with Papua New Guinea* (Sydney: Australian Broadcasting Commission, 2001), 147.
3. *Papa graun*: father of the ground or land in Tok Pisin.
4. *Mumu*: earth oven.
5. *Tanget*: a shrub (*Cordyline fructicosa* species of plant) whose leaves are used in sorcery for sending messages and as a mnemonic device by knots made into them.

Fording the troubled ocean of *saṃsāra**

Mysore Hiriyanna†

The beginnings of Indian philosophy take us very far back indeed, for we can clearly trace them in the hymns of the Ṛgveda which were composed by the Aryans not long after they had settled in their new home about the middle of the second millennium before Christ. The speculative activity begun so early was continued till a century or two ago, so that the history that we have to narrate in the following pages covers a period of over thirty centuries. During this long period, Indian thought developed practically unaffected by outside influence; and the extent as well as the importance of its achievements will be evident when we mention that it has evolved several systems of philosophy, besides creating a great national religion—Brahminism, and a great world religion—Buddhism. The history of so unique a development, if it could be written in full, would be of immense value; but our knowledge at present of early India, in spite of the remarkable results achieved by modern research, is too meagre and imperfect for it. Not only can we not trace the growth of single philosophic ideas step by step; we are sometimes unable to determine the relation even between one system

---

* An extract from Mysore Hiriyanna's seminal work based on his lecture notes, *Outlines of Indian Philosophy* (London: George Allen & Unwin Ltd, 1932), 13-26. This text is in the public domain.

† Mysore Hiriyanna (1871-1950) was an Indian philosopher and Professor of Sanskrit at the University of Mysore. He held an MA from Madras Christian College and lived in Mysore, India.

and another. Thus it remains a moot question to this day whether the Sāṅkhya represents an original doctrine or is only derived from some other. This deficiency is due as much to our ignorance of significant details as to an almost total lack of exact chronology in early Indian history. The only date that can be claimed to have been settled in the first one thousand years of it, for example, is that of the death of Buddha, which occurred in 487 B.C. Even the dates we know in the subsequent portion of it are for the most part conjectural, so that the very limits of the periods under which we propose to treat of our subject are to be regarded as tentative. Accordingly our account, it will be seen, is characterised by a certain looseness of perspective. In this connection we may also perhaps refer to another of its drawbacks which is sure to strike a student who is familiar with *Histories* of European philosophy. Our account will for the most part be devoid of references to the lives or character of the great thinkers with whose teaching it is concerned, for very little of them is now known. Speaking of Udayana, an eminent Nyāya thinker, Cowell wrote:[1] 'He shines like one of the fixed stars in India's literary firmament, but no telescope can discover any appreciable diameter; his name is a *point* of light, but we can detect therein nothing that belongs to our earth or material existence.' That description applies virtually to all who were responsible for the development of Indian thought; and even a great teacher like Śaṅkara is to us now hardly more than a name. It has been suggested[2] that this indifference on the part of the ancient Indians towards the personal histories of their great men was due to a realisation by them that individuals are but the product of their times—'that they grow from a soil that is ready-made for them and breathe an intellectual atmosphere which is not of their own making.' It was perhaps not less the result of the humble sense which those great men had of themselves. But whatever the reason, we shall miss in our account the biographical background and all the added interest which it signifies.

If we take the date given above as a landmark, we may divide the history of Indian thought into two stages. It marks the close of the Vedic period[3] and the beginning of what is known as the Sanskrit or classical period. To the former belong the numerous works that are regarded by the Hindus as revealed. These works, which in extent have been compared to 'what survives of the writings of ancient Greece,' were collected in the latter part of the period. If we overlook the changes that should have crept into them before they were thus brought together, they have been preserved, owing mainly to the fact that they were held sacred, with remarkable accuracy; and they are consequently far more authentic than any work of such antiquity can be expected to be. But the collection, because it was made chiefly, as we shall see, for ritualistic purposes, is incomplete and therefore fails to give us a full insight into the character of the thoughts and beliefs that existed then. The works appear in it arranged in a way, but the arrangement is not such as would be of use to us here; and the collection is from our present standpoint to be viewed as lacking in system. As regards the second period, we possess a yet more extensive literature; and, since new manuscripts continue to be discovered, additions to it are still being made. The information it furnishes is accordingly fuller and more diverse. Much of this material also appears in a systematised form. But this literature cannot always be considered quite as authentic as the earlier one, for in the course of long oral transmission, which was once the recognised mode of handing down knowledge, many of the old treatises have received additions or been amended while they have retained their original titles. The systematic treatises among them even in their original form, do not carry us back to the beginning of the period. Some of them are undoubtedly very old, but even they are not as old as 500 B.C., to state that limit in round numbers. It means that the post-Vedic period is itself to be split up into two stages. If for the purpose of this book we designate the later of them as 'the age of the systems,' we are left with an intervening period which for want of a better title may be described as 'the early post-Vedic period.' Its duration is not precisely determinable, but it lasted sufficiently long—from 500 B.C. to about the beginning of the Christian era—to be viewed as a distinct stage in the growth of Indian thought. It marks a transition and its literature, as may be expected, partakes of the character of the literatures of the preceding and of the succeeding periods. While it is many-sided and not fully authentic like its successor, it is unsystematised like its predecessor.

Leaving the details of our subject, so far as they fall within the scope of this work, to be recounted in the following chapters, we may devote the present to a general survey of it. A striking characteristic of Indian thought is its richness and variety. There is practically no shade of speculation which it does not include. This is a matter that is often lost sight of by its present-day critic who is fond of applying to it sweeping epithets like 'negative' and 'pessimistic' which, though not incorrect so far as some of its phases are concerned, are altogether misleading as descriptions of it as a whole. There is, as will become clear when we study our subject in its several stages of growth, no lack of emphasis on the reality of the external world or on the optimistic view of life understood in its larger sense. The misconception is largely due to the partial knowledge of Indian thought which hitherto prevailed; for it was not till recently that works on Indian philosophy, which deal with it in anything like a comprehensive manner, were published. The schools of thought familiarly known till then were only a few; and even in their case, it was forgotten that they do not stand for a uniform doctrine throughout their history, but exhibit important modifications rendering such wholesale descriptions of them inaccurate. The fact is that Indian thought exhibits such a diversity of development that it does not admit of a rough-and-ready characterisation. Underlying this varied development, there are two divergent currents clearly discernible—one having its source in the Veda and the other, independent of it. We might describe them as orthodox and heterodox respectively, provided we remember that these terms are only relative and that either school may designate the other as heterodox, claiming for itself the 'halo of orthodoxy.' The second of these currents is the later, for it commences as a reaction against the first; but it is not much later since it manifests itself quite early as shown by references to it even in the Vedic hymns. It appears originally as critical and negative; but it begins before long to develop a constructive side which is of great consequence in the history of Indian philosophy. Broadly speaking, it is pessimistic and realistic. The other doctrine cannot be described thus briefly, for even in its earliest recorded phase it presents a very complex character. While for example the prevailing spirit of the songs included in the Ṛgveda is optimistic, there is sometimes a note of sadness in them as in those addressed to the goddess of Dawn (Uṣas), which pointedly refer to the way in which she cuts short the little lives of men. 'Obeying the behests of the gods, but wasting away the lives of mortals, Uṣas has shone forth—the last of many former dawns and the first of those that are yet to come.'[4] The characteristic marks of the two currents are, however, now largely obliterated owing to the assimilation or appropriation of the doctrines of each by the other during a long period of contact; but the distinction itself has not disappeared and can be seen in the Vedānta and Jainism, both of which are still living creeds.

These two types of thought, though distinct in their origin and general spirit, exhibit certain common features. We shall dwell at some length upon them, as they form the basic principles of Indian philosophy considered as a whole:—

(i) The first of them has in recent times become the subject of a somewhat commonplace observation, *viz*. that religion and philosophy do not stand sundered in India. They indeed begin as one everywhere, for their purpose is in the last resort the same, *viz*. a seeking for the central meaning of existence. But soon they separate and develop on more or less different lines. In India also the differentiation takes place, but only it does not mean divorce. This result has in all probability been helped by the isolated development of Indian thought already referred to,[5] and has generally been recognised as a striking excellence of it. But owing to the vagueness of the word 'religion,' we may easily miss the exact significance of the observation. This word, as it is well known, may stand for anything ranging from what has been described as 'a sum of scruples which impede the free use of our faculties' to a yearning of the human spirit for union with God. It is no praise to any philosophy to be associated with religion in the former sense. Besides, some Indian doctrines are not religion at all in the commonly accepted sense. For example, early Buddhism was avowedly atheistic and it did not recognise any permanent spirit. Yet the statement that religion and philosophy have been one in India is apparently intended to be applicable to all the doctrines. So it is necessary to find out in what sense of the word the observation in question is true. Whatever else a religion may or may not be, it is essentially a reaching forward to an ideal, without resting in mere belief or outward observances. Its distinctive mark is that it serves to further right living; and it is only in this sense that we can speak of religion as one with philosophy in India.[6] The ancient Indian did not stop short at the discovery of truth, but strove to realise it in his own experience. He followed up *tattva-jñāna*, as it is termed, by a strenuous effort to attain *mokṣa* or liberation,[7] which therefore, and not merely an intellectual conviction, was in his view the real goal of philosophy. In the words of Max Müller, philosophy was recommended in India 'not for the sake of knowledge, but for the highest purpose that man can strive after in this life.'[8] The conception of *mokṣa* varies from system to system; but it marks, according to all, the culmination of philosophic culture. In other words, Indian philosophy aims beyond Logic. This peculiarity of the view-point is to be ascribed to the fact that philosophy in India did not take its rise in wonder or curiosity as it seems to have done in the West; rather it originated under the pressure of a practical need arising from the presence of moral and physical evil in life. It is the problem of how to remove this evil that troubled the ancient Indian most, and *mokṣa* in all the systems represents a state in which it is, in one sense or another, taken to have been overcome. Philosophic endeavour was directed primarily to find a remedy for the ills of life, and the consideration of metaphysical questions came in as a matter of course. This is clearly indicated for instance by the designation—sometimes applied to the founders of the several schools—of '*Tīrtha-kara*' or '*Tīrthaṅ-kara*,' which literally means 'ford-maker' and signifies one that has discovered the way to the other shore across the troubled ocean of *saṃsāra*.

But it may be thought that the idea of *mokṣa*, being eschatological, rests on mere speculation and that, though it may be regarded as the goal of faith, it can hardly be represented as that of philosophy. Really, however, there is no ground for thinking so, for, thanks to the constant presence in the Indian mind of a positivistic standard, the *mokṣa* ideal, even in those schools in which it was not so from the outset, speedily came to be conceived as realisable in this life, and described as *jīvan-mukti*, or emancipation while yet alive. It still remained, no doubt, a distant ideal; but what is important to note is that it ceased to be regarded as something to be reached in a life beyond. Man's aim was no longer represented as the attainment of perfection in a hypothetical hereafter, but as a continual progress towards it within the limits of the present life. Even in the case of doctrines like the Nyāya-Vaiśeṣika[9] or the Viśiṣṭādvaita[10] which do not formally accept the *jīvan-mukti* ideal, there is clearly recognised the possibility of man reaching here a state of enlightenment which may justifiably be so described because it completely transforms his outlook upon the world and fills with an altogether new significance the life he thereafter leads in it. Such an ideal was already part and parcel of a very influential doctrine in the latter part of the Vedic period, for it is found in the Upaniṣads. One of these ancient treatises says: 'When all the desires the heart harbours are gone, man becomes immortal and reaches Brahman *here*.'[11] It points beyond intellectual satisfaction, which is often mistaken to be the aim of philosophy, and yet by keeping within the bounds of possible human experience avoids the dogma of *mokṣa* in the eschatological sense. The latter view also, known as *videhamukti*, has survived, but it is a relic from earlier times when it was believed that the consequences of a good or bad life led here were to be reaped elsewhere in a state beyond death: and the retention of it by any school does not really affect its philosophic standpoint.

(ii) A necessary corollary to such a view of the goal of philosophy is the laying down of a suitable course of practical discipline for its attainment. Philosophy thereby becomes a way of life, not merely a way of thought. It has been remarked with reference to Jainism that its fundamental maxim is 'Do not live to know, but know to live'[12] and the same may well be said of the other Indian schools also.[13] The discipline naturally varies in the two traditions; but there is underlying it in both an ascetic spirit whose inculcation

Fording the troubled ocean of saṃsāra

is another common characteristic of all Indian doctrines.[14] Sureśvara, a famous disciple of Śaṅkara, remarks[15] that, though systems of thought including heretical ones like Buddhism may differ in the substance of their theories, they are all at one in teaching renunciation. It means that while agreeing with one another in regard to the necessity of renunciation, they assign different reasons for it. That the heretical systems which in general were pessimistic should have commended absolute detachment is quite intelligible, for they were pervaded by a belief in the vanity and nothingness of life. What is specially noteworthy here is that the orthodox schools also, some of which at least were optimistic, should have done the same. But there is a very important difference between asceticism as taught in the two schools. The heterodox held that man should once for all turn away from the world whatever his circumstances might be. But the orthodox regarded the ascetic ideal as only to be progressively realised. As Dr. Winternitz observes,[16] it is in their opinion to be approached 'only from the point of view of the āśrama theory according to which the Aryan has first to pass the state of Brahmacārin, the student of the Veda, and of the householder (gṛhastha) who founds a family, offers sacrifices and honours the Brāhmaṇas, before he is allowed to retire from this world as a hermit or an ascetic.' The contrast between the two ideals is set forth in a striking manner in a chapter of the Mahābhārata known as the 'Dialogue between Father and Son.'[17] Here the father, who represents the orthodox view, maintains that renunciation should come at the end of the *āśrama* discipline, but is won over to his side by the son, who holds the view that it is the height of unwisdom to follow amidst the many uncertainties of life such dilatory discipline and pleads for an immediate breaking away from all worldly ties.[18] That is, detachment according to the former cannot be acquired without a suitable preliminary training undergone in the midst of society; but, according to the latter, it can be achieved at once, any moment of disillusionment about the world sufficing for it. The one believes social training to be indispensable[19] for the perfection of character; the other looks upon it as more a hindrance than a help to it. But the social factor, it should be added, is disregarded by the heterodox only as a means of self-culture, and their attitude towards it is neither one of revulsion nor one of neglect. For we know as a matter of fact that they attached the greatest value to society in itself and laid particular stress upon the need for sympathy and kindness for fellow-men. There are other differences as well such as the pursuit of ascetic morality by the heterodox, as the sole mode of practical discipline, and by the orthodox as only a preparation for a fresh course of training which may itself be different in different schools. But whatever the differences in matters of detail, asceticism as such serves as a bond of union between the two traditions. Even systems which do not at first appear to countenance it are, as a little reflection will show, really favourable to it. Thus ritualism with its promise of prosperity in a world to come actually results in complete self-denial so far as this world is concerned, because the fruit of the deeds it prescribes is to be reaped not here, but elsewhere and amidst conditions totally different from those of the present life. The principle of detachment implicit in such doctrines was, as we shall see, rendered explicit, and even the ulterior motive of self-love which is involved in striving for reward hereafter was eliminated by the Gītā with its teaching of disinterested action.

Owing to the spirit of renunciation that runs through them all, the way of life which the Indian doctrines prescribe may be characterised as aiming at transcending morality as commonly understood. In other words, the goal of Indian philosophy lies as much beyond Ethics as it does beyond Logic. As however the *rationale* of the ascetic ideal is explained in two different ways by Indian thinkers, the supermoral attitude bears a somewhat different significance in the several schools; but this distinction does not, like the previous one, correspond to the division into orthodox and heterodox traditions. Some schools admit the ultimacy of the individual self while others deny it in one sense or another. Buddhism for example altogether repudiates the individual self as a permanent entity, while Absolutism takes it as eventually merging in the true or universal self so that its individuality is only provisional. Theism on the other hand like that of Rāmānuja and pluralistic systems like Jainism or the Nyāya-Vaiśeṣika recognise the individual self to be ultimate, but point out that the way to deliverance lies only through the annihilation of egoism (*ahaṅ-kāra*). Now according to the systems which deny the individual self in one form or another, the very notion of obligation ceases to be significant finally, the contrast between the individual and society upon which that notion is based being entirely negated in it. Referring to a person that has attained to such a super-individual outlook, the *Taittirīya Upaniṣad* says[20]: 'He is not troubled by thoughts like these: Have I not done the right? Have I done the wrong?' In the other systems which admit the ultimacy of the individual self but teach the necessity for absolute self-suppression, the consciousness of obligation continues, but the disciple devotes himself to its fulfilment with no thought whatsoever of his rights. That is, though the contrast between the individual and society is felt, that between rights and duties disappears; and so far, the motive is lifted above that of common morality. According to both the views, the essential duality of the moral world is transcended on account of the total renunciation of personal interest; in neither is it merely an adjustment, however difficult or delicate, of rights and duties between the individual and his social environment.

There is a sense, we may add, in which the practical training, even in its preliminary stages, may be said to aim at transcending morality as ordinarily conceived. The individual's obligations, according to the Indian view, are not confined to human society, but extend to virtually the whole of sentient creation. To the common precept 'Love thy neighbour as thyself,' it adds, as has been observed by one than whom nobody now is better fitted to interpret the Indian ideal of life, 'And every living being is thy neighbour.'[21] Such an extension of the world of moral action accords well with the spirit of Indian ethics whose watchword is devotion to duties rather than assertion of rights. Beings that are not characterised by moral consciousness may have no duties to fulfil, but it does not mean that there is none to be fulfilled towards them. This ideal of the fellowship of all living beings is best illustrated by the principle of non-injury (*ahiṅsā*), which forms an integral part of every one of the higher Indian faiths and was practised not only by saints and sages, but also by emperors like Aśoka. It may minimise the importance of human society. That is because the ideal has not less regard for it but more for the wider whole which comprehends all animate being. It does not thereby ignore the spirit of human unity. Only it conceives of that spirit as consisting not in striving for human well-being alone, but also in discharging towards all living creatures the obligation corresponding to the position of privilege which mankind occupies in the scheme of the universe. Social morality, however much it may widen our outlook from the individual's standpoint, really keeps us isolated from the rest of creation. In addition to personal egoism, there is what may be called the egoism of the species which leads inevitably to the belief that the sub-human world may be exploited for the benefit of man. That also must be got rid of, if man is to become truly free; and he will do so only when he has risen above the anthropocentric view and can look upon everything as equally sacred—whether it be, in the words of the Gītā,[22] 'a cow or elephant or dog, the cultured Brahmin or the outcaste that feeds on dogs.'

These are the two elements common to all Indian thought—the pursuit of *mokṣa* as the final ideal and the ascetic spirit of the discipline recommended for its attainment. They signify that philosophy as understood in India is neither mere intellectualism nor mere moralism, but includes and transcends them both. In other words it aims, as already stated, at achieving more than what Logic and Ethics can. But it must not be forgotten that, though not themselves constituting the end, these are the *sole* means of approach to it. They have been represented as the two wings that help the soul in its spiritual flight. The goal that is reached through their aid is characterised on the one hand by *jñāna* or illumination which is intellectual conviction that has ripened into an immediate experience and, on the other, by *vairāgya* or self-renunciation which is secure by reason of the discovery of the Metaphysical ground for it. It is pre-eminently an attitude of peace which does not necessarily imply passivity. But the emphasis is on the attitude itself or on the inward experience that gives rise to it, rather than on the outward behaviour which is looked upon as its expression and therefore more or less secondary. The value of philosophic training lies as little in inducing a person to do what otherwise he would not have done, as in instructing him in what otherwise he would not have known; it consists essentially in making him what he was not before. Heaven, it has been remarked, is first a temperament and then anything else.

We have so far spoken about the main divisions of Indian tradition, which, though exhibiting certain common features, are fundamentally different. The history of Indian philosophy is the history of the ways in which the two traditions have acted and reacted upon each other, giving rise to divergent schools of thought. Their mutual influence, however much desirable as the means of broadening the basis of thought, has led to a considerable overlapping of the two sets of doctrines, rendering it difficult to discover what elements each has incorporated from the other. It is impossible, for instance, to say for certain to which of the two traditions we owe the ideal of *jīvan-mukti* to whose importance we have drawn attention. In the course of this progressive movement, now one school and now another was in the ascendant. The ascendancy at one stage belonged conspicuously to Buddhism, and it seemed as if it had once for all gained the upper hand. But finally the Vedānta triumphed. It has naturally been transformed much in the process, although its inner character remains as it was already foreshadowed in the Upaniṣads. We may indeed regard the several phases in the history of the heretical tradition as only so many steps leading to this final development. The Vedānta may accordingly be taken to represent the consummation of Indian thought, and in it we may truly look for the highest type of the Indian ideal. On the theoretical side, it stands for the triumph of Absolutism and Theism, for whatever differences may characterise the various Vedāntic schools, they are classifiable under these two heads. The former is monistic and the latter, though avowedly pluralistic, may also be said to be governed by the spirit of monism owing to the emphasis it places on the entire dependence of everything on God. On the practical side, the triumph of the Vedānta has meant the triumph of the positive ideal of life. This is shown not only by the social basis of the ethical discipline which the Vedānta as an orthodox doctrine commends, but also by its conception of the highest good which consists, as we shall see when we come to consider the several sys-

Synkrētic

tems in detail, not in isolating the self from its environment as it does for the heterodox schools but in overcoming the opposition between the two by identifying the interests of the self with those of the whole. Both ideals alike involve the cultivation of complete detachment; but the detachment in the case of the Vedānta is of a higher and finer type. Kālidāsa, who, as the greatest of Indian poets, may be expected to have given the truest expression to the ideal of practical life known to the Indians, describes it[23] as 'owning the whole world while disowning oneself.' The Vedāntic idea of the highest good also implies the recognition of a cosmic purpose, whether that purpose be conceived as ordained by God or as inherent in the nature of Reality itself, towards whose fulfilment everything consciously or unconsciously moves. The heretical schools, except in so far as they have been influenced by the other ideal, do not see any such purpose in the world as a whole, though they admit the possibility of the individual freeing himself from evil.

Notes

1 Introduction to *Kusumāñjali* (Eng. Translation), pp. v and vi.
2 SS. p. 2.
3 It is usual to state the lower limit of the Vedic period as 200 B.C., including within it works which, though not regarded as 'revealed' (*śruti*), are yet exclusively concerned with the elucidation of revealed texts. We are here confining the term strictly to the period in which Vedic works appeared.
4 *Cf.* RV. I. 124. 2.
5 We may perhaps instance as a contrast the course which thought has taken in Europe, where the tradition of classical culture, which is essentially Indo-European, has mingled with a Semitic creed. Mrs. Rhys Davids speaks of science, philosophy and religion as being 'in an armed truce' in the West. See *Buddhism* (Home University Library), p. 100.
6 Indian philosophy may show alliance with religion in other senses also, but such alliance does not form a common characteristic of all the doctrines.
7 *Cf.* NS. I. i. 3.
8 SS. p. 370.

9   See NSB. IV. ii. 2; NV. I. i. 1. *ad finem*.
10 See SB. IV. i. 13.
11 *Kaṭha Up*, II. iii. 14.
12 OJ. p. 112.
13 Compare in this connection Professor Whitehead's characterisation of Buddhism as 'the most colossal example in history of applied metaphysics': *Religion in the Making*, p. 39.
14 The Cārvāka view is an exception; but it is hardly a system of philosophy in the form in which it is now known. See Ch. VIII.
15 BUV. pp. 513-15. st. 405-411.
16 'Ascetic Literature in Ancient India': *Calcutta University Review* for October 1923, p. 3.
17 xii. 277.
18 This does not mean that there is no place for the laity in heterodox society, but only that lay training is not viewed as obligatory before one becomes a monk.
19 The rule relating to the discipline of the *āśrama* was, as we shall see in a subsequent chapter, much relaxed in later times by the orthodox; but even thus the option to become an ascetic is to be exercised only after one has passed through the first stage of *brahma-carya*. It should also be stated that the relaxation, to judge from current practice, is mostly in theory and that early renunciation is the exception, not the rule.
20 ii. 9.
21 See Romain Rolland: *Mahatma Gandhi*, p. 33.
22 v. 18.
23 *Mālavikāgnimitram*, i. 1.

The philosophy of redemption*

Philipp Mainländer[†]

TRANSLATED BY *Christian Romuss*[‡]

Whoever investigates the course of the human mind's development, from the beginning of civilisation up to our own day, shall make a curious discovery. He shall find, namely, that reason at first grasped nature's undeniable power always in a fragmented manner and personified the discrete expressions of force, that is, formed gods; then melded these gods into a single God; then, by means of the most abstract thought, made this God into a being that could no longer be imagined in any way; finally, however, became critical, tore up its own subtle fabrication, and set the real individual—the fact of inner and outer experience—on the throne.

The stations of this path are:

    1) polytheism;
    2) monotheism – pantheism:
        a. religious pantheism,

---

* These extracts are taken from a translation of the first volume of Philipp Mainländer's *Die Philosophie der Erlösung* (1876), which will be published under the English title *The Philosophy of Redemption* by Irukandji Press in 2023. The extracts are taken from the foreword and the chapters on physics and metaphysics. They have been edited for coherence.

† Philipp Mainländer (1841-1876), born Philipp Batz, was a German philosopher and poet. He trained as a merchant and was largely self-taught in literature and philosophy. He lived in Offenbach am Main, Naples, and Berlin.

‡ Christian Romuss is Deputy Editor of *Synkrētic*. He holds a PhD in the History of Ideas from the University of Queensland. He translates German and Spanish philosophy. He is based in Brisbane, Australia.

  b. philosophical pantheism;
 3) atheism.

 Not all civilisations have walked the entire path. The mental life of most has halted at the first or second point of development, and only in two countries has the final station been reached: in India and in Judea.

 The religion of the Indians was initially polytheism, then pantheism. (Later, very refined and eminent minds took possession of religious pantheism and developed it into philosophical pantheism—Vedanta philosophy.) At this juncture, Buddha, the glorious prince, appeared, and in his sublime doctrine of karma he founded atheism on *faith* in the *omnipotence* of the individual.

 Likewise, the religion of the Jews was at first crude polytheism, then strict monotheism. In monotheism as in pantheism, the individual lost his final trace of autonomy. As Schopenhauer very aptly remarks: Having sufficiently tormented his utterly powerless creature, Jehovah then threw it on the dung heap. Against this, critical reason reacted with unbridled force in the exalted personality of Christ. Christ restored the individual once more to his inalienable right, and on that right, and on *faith* in the motion of the world out of life into death (downfall of the world), he founded the atheistic religion of redemption. That pure Christianity in its deepest foundation is genuine atheism (*i.e.*, *denial* of a *personal* God *coexisting* with the world, but *affirmation* of an immense, all-pervading breath sighed out by a godhead *which perished before it*) and only on its surface is monotheism, I shall prove in this work.

 Exoteric Christianity became a world religion and, following its triumph, not a single civilisation more reached the endpoint of the developmental course described above.

 In contrast, in the community of Western nations, Western philosophy advanced alongside the Christian religion and is now approaching the third station. It took its lead from Aristotelian philosophy, which was preceded by the Ionian. In the latter, discrete *visible* individualities of the world (water, air, fire) were made into principles of the whole, in a manner similar to that of every primitive religion, wherein discrete observed agencies of nature were formed into gods. In the Middle Ages (pure Christianity had already gone astray long before), the simple unity which had been gained in Aristotelian philosophy through the condensation of all forms then became the philosophically pruned God of the Christian Church; for Scholasticism is nothing other than philosophical monotheism.

This monotheism then metamorphosed through Scotus Erigena, Vanini, Bruno, and Spinoza into philosophical pantheism, which, under the influence of a particular branch of philosophy (that is, of critical idealism: Locke, Berkeley, Hume, Kant) was shaped further: on one hand, into pantheism without process (Schopenhauer), and, on the other, into pantheism with development (Schelling, Hegel). That is, it was driven to extremes.

Most of the educated people of all civilised nations whose foundation is Western culture presently move within this philosophical pantheism (it is all the same whether the simple unity which pervades the world be called will or idea, or matter or the absolute)—just as the noble Indians did at the time of Vedanta philosophy. But now the day of reaction has come.

The individual demands, louder than ever, the restoration of his torn up and trampled but inalienable right.

This work is the first attempt to give him that right unconditionally.

The philosophy of redemption is the continuation of the doctrines of Kant and of Schopenhauer, and the confirmation of Buddhism and of pure Christianity. It amends and supplements those philosophical systems, and reconciles these religions with science.

As a philosophy it founds atheism not on some faith, as these religions do, but on *scientific knowledge*, and so, for the first time, atheism has been given a scientific foundation.

Atheism will also become part of the scientific knowledge of humanity, for humanity is ripe for it. Humanity has come of age.

♦

The first motion and the arising of the world are one and the same. The transformation of the simple unity into the world of multiplicity, the transition from the transcendent to the immanent domain, was precisely this first motion. It is not the task of physics to explain the first motion; physics has to accept it as a fact that has been found already in the Analytics, in the immanent domain but close to the boundary of the transcendent, which is added on in thought. This is why even in the Physics the final expression for this first motion cannot be gained, and we must simply characterise it, from our current perspective, as the disintegration of the simple unity into a world of multiplicity.

All subsequent motions were only continuations of this first motion, *i.e.*, they could not be anything other than, again, the disintegration or further fragmentation of the ideas.

In the first ages of the world, this further disintegration was only able to express itself through real division of the simple substances and through being compounded. Every simple chemical force was obsessed with extending its individuality, *i.e.*, with modifying its motion, but in every other force it stumbled upon the same obsession, and so arose the most terrible struggles of the ideas against each other in the most intense, excited states. The result was always a chemical compounding, *i.e.*, the victory of the stronger over a weaker force and the entry of the new idea into the ceaseless struggle. The striving of the compound was at first directed at maintaining itself, then, when possible, at extending its individuality further. But against both strivings there entered from all sides other ideas, first to dissolve the compound, then to compound themselves with the divided ideas.

In the continuation of this ceaseless fight of the imperishable ideas which lay at the foundation of all compounds, the celestial bodies were formed, of which our earth gradually became ripe for organic life. If we here interrupt our development and take the present individuals and their states as final products, then the question immediately forces itself upon us: What has happened? All the ideas from which our earth was composed at that time were in the fiery primordial nebula on which the Kantian-Laplacian theory is based. There a wild struggle of gases, vapours, chaos; here a closed world-body with a solid crust whose depths were filled by a hot sea; and above all of it a vaporous, nebulous, carbon-dioxide-containing atmosphere.

What has happened? Or better: Are the individual wills of which this earth is constituted, this earth which has been liberated from becoming, the very same wills which spun in the fiery primordial nebula? Certainly! The *genetic* context is there. But is the *essence* of some individuality still the same one that it was at the beginning of the world? No! It has changed. Its force has *lost intensity*. It has become *weaker*.

This is the great truth taught by geology. A gas, according to its innermost essence, its drive, is stronger than a liquid and this in turn is stronger than a solid body. Let us not forget that the world has a *finite* sphere of force, and that for this reason some idea or other, whose intensity abates, cannot be strengthened again without another idea losing force. A strengthening is nevertheless possible but always at the expense of another force, or in other words: If, in the struggle of the inorganic ideas, one of these is weakened, then the objectified sum of forces in the universe is weakened, and for this deficiency there is no substitute precisely because the world is finite and came into existence with a particular force.

If we therefore assume that our earth should one day explode like that planet between Mars and Jupiter which broke into pieces, then the entire solid crust of the earth can certainly melt again and all liquid become vapour, but at the cost of the ideas which provide the stimuli to such events. Thus, even if the earth were thrown back into what seemed a more intense state by means of such a revolution, it has still become *weaker as a whole*, as a particular sum of force.

And if today the powerful processes on the sun ceased and all the bodies of our solar system were thereby reunited with the sun, and sun and planets blazed up in an immense celestial fire, then it would seem that the forces that constitute the solar system had transformed into a more excited state, but at the expense of the total force contained in our solar system.

Even now it is no different in the inorganic realm. The ideas struggle ceaselessly with each other. Without interruption new compounds arise and these are violently divided again, but the divided forces unite with others straight away, partly compelling the union, partly being compelled into it. And here, too, the result is *weakening of force*, although this result, because of its slow development, lies not in the plain light of day, and eludes perception.

In the organic realm, from the moment it arose, there reigned and reigns evermore as a continuation of the first motion: disintegration into multiplicity. The striving of every organism is directed merely towards maintaining itself in existence and, following this drive, it struggles on one hand for its existence and provides on the other hand, by means of procreation, for its maintenance after death.

That this growing fragmentation on one hand and the struggle for existence that thereby becomes more intense and terrible on the other must have the same result as the struggle in the inorganic realm—namely, weakening of the individuals—is clear. The fact that the strongest individual (in the broadest sense) remains the victor in the struggle for existence and the weaker individual surrenders only seems to speak against this fact; for the stronger may usually gain the victory, to be sure, but in every new generation the stronger individuals are less strong, the weaker individuals weaker than those in the previous generation.

We thus see in the organic as in the inorganic realm a fundamental motion: disintegration into multiplicity, and in the former as in the latter we see as the first consequence: conflict, struggle and war, and as the second consequence: the weakening of force. But the disintegration into multiplicity as well as the two consequences of this disintegration are in every respect greater in the organic realm than in the inorganic.

Here the questions are forced upon us: In what relations do the two realms stand to each other? And is there between both really a chasm that cannot be bridged?

Now, in physics, as we know, the first motion presents itself as disintegration of the transcendent unity into multiplicity. All motions that followed it bear the same character. Disintegration into multiplicity, life, motion—all of these expressions describe one and the same thing. The disintegration of unity into multiplicity is the fundamental law in the inorganic as well as the organic realm. In the latter, however, it finds a much more extensive application: it cuts much deeper, and its consequences—the struggle for existence and the weakening of force—are greater.

No chasm [therefore] separates the inorganic bodies from organisms. The organic realm is only a higher rung of the inorganic; it is a *more complete form* of the struggle for existence, *i.e.*, of the *weakening of force*.

As frightful, indeed as ludicrous as it may sound to say that man is fundamentally a chemical compound and differs from such a compound only insofar as he has a different motion, it is yet a true result of the Physics. It loses its repellent character when one keeps firmly in view the fact that wherever one may investigate nature, one always finds but one principle, the individual will, which wants only one thing: to live, to live. The essence of a stone is simpler than that of a lion, but only on the surface; fundamentally it is the same: individual will-to-life.

By tracing the organic realm back to the inorganic, immanent philosophy does indeed teach the same thing as materialism, but it is not for that reason identical with materialism. The fundamental difference which exists between them is the following.

Materialism is no *immanent* philosophical system. The first thing that it teaches is *eternal matter*, a *simple unity*, which no one has yet seen, and no one shall ever see. If materialism wanted to be immanent, *i.e.*, *merely* to be honest in the contemplation of nature, then above all it would have to declare matter to be a *collective* unity independent of the Subject and say that matter is the *sum* of so and so many simple substances. This, however, it does not do, and although no one has yet succeeded in making hydrogen from oxygen, gold from copper, materialism yet places *behind* every simple substance the mystical simple essentiality: undifferentiated matter. Neither Zeus nor Jupiter, neither the God of the Jews, Christians, and Mohammedans, nor the Brahma of the Indians, in short: no uncognisable, transcendent essentiality has been so devoutly believed in from the depths of the human heart as that mystical divinity of the materialists: matter.

However, despite the extraordinary assumption of simple matter, an assumption which strikes all experience in the face, it is yet insufficient to explain the world. Thus, once again, materialism must deny the truth, once again it must wax transcendent and posit various mystical essences, the forces of nature, which are not identical with matter and yet are connected with it for all time. In this way, materialism rests on *two* primordial principles, or in other words: it is *transcendent dogmatic dualism*.

In immanent philosophy, by contrast, matter is *ideal*, in our heads, a subjective capacity which enables us to cognise the external world, and *substance*, though an *undifferentiated unity*, is in the same sense *ideal*, in our heads, a conjunction à posteriori gained by synthetic reason on the basis of matter, without the slightest reality and existing only in order to cognise *all* objects.

Independently of the Subject there is only *force*, only individual will in the world: a single principle.

Therefore, whereas materialism is transcendent dogmatic dualism, immanent philosophy is *pure, immanent dynamism*: a difference than which no greater can be conceived.

To call materialism the *most rational* system is thoroughly absurd. Every transcendent system is eo ipso *not* rational. Materialism, conceived only as a theoretical system of philosophy, is worse than its reputation. The truth that the simple chemical ideas are the sea from which everything organic has emerged, from which it arises and into which it sinks back, casts a purely immanent light on materialism and thereby gives it a seductive charm. But critical reason does not allow itself to be deceived. It investigates precisely, and thus finds behind the dazzling illusion that old chimera: the transcendent unity in or above or under the world and coexisting with it, which appears now in this, now in that, but always in fantastical attire.

In the Analytics we defined the character of the premundane simple unity negatively in accordance with the faculties of cognition. We found this unity to be inactive, extensionless, undifferentiated, unfragmented (simple), motionless, timeless (eternal). We have now to define it from the standpoint of the Physics.

Whatever kind of Object of nature we may contemplate, be it a gas, a liquid, a stone, a plant, an animal, a man, we always find it in relentless striving, in a ceaseless inner motion. To the transcendent unity, however, motion was foreign. The opposite of motion is rest, of which we can form for ourselves no notion; for we are not here speaking of apparent *external* rest, which in relation to the change of location of an entire Object or parts of the same we are indeed very much in a position to imagine, but of inner, absolute motionlessness. We must therefore attribute *absolute rest* to the premundane unity.

If we then reflect seriously on the dynamic coherence of the universe on one hand and on the definite character of the individuals on the other, then we recognise that everything in the world moves of *necessity*. Whatever we may contemplate: the stone dropped by our hand, the growing plant, the animal that moves upon intuitive motives and inner compulsion, the man who must surrender himself without resistance to a sufficient motive—they all are subject to the iron law of necessity. In the world there is no room for freedom. And, as we will see clearly in the Ethics, it must be so if the world is to have a sense at all.

What freedom is in a philosophical sense (liberum arbitrium indifferentiae) we can indeed define with words and say, for example, that it is the capacity of a man of a particular character to will or not to will in the face of a sufficient motive; but if we also reflect but a moment on this combination of words which is so easily contrived, then we recognise immediately that we will never obtain real evidence of this freedom, even if it were possible for us to examine the actions of all men to their very foundation over millennia. For us it is therefore with freedom as it is with rest. But we must attribute freedom to the simple unity, precisely because it was a simple unity. With it the compulsion of motive, the one factor of every motion known to us, falls away, for the unity was unfragmented, entirely alone, solitary.

The immanent scheme:

world of multiplicity – motion – necessity

is therefore paralleled by the transcendent scheme:

simple unity – rest – freedom.

And now we must take the final step.

In the Analytics we already found that *force*, as soon as it has passed via the thin thread of existence from the immanent into the transcendent domain, ceases to be *force*. It becomes for us as completely unfamiliar and uncognisable as the unity into which it becomes submerged. As we proceeded in that chapter, we found that what we call force is *individual will*, and in the Physics we have finally seen that the *mind* is only the function of an organ that has precipitated from the will and in its deepest foundation is nothing other than a part of a divided motion.

The fundamental principle, the will, which is so intimate, so well-known to us in the immanent domain, and the secondary principle which is subordinated to it and likewise so intimate, the mind, lose (like force) all meaning for us as soon as we allow them to pass over to the transcendent domain. They forfeit their nature completely and elude our cognition entirely.

We are therefore compelled to conclude that the simple unity was neither *will*, nor *mind*, nor an idiosyncratic *interpenetration of will and mind*. In this way we lose our final point of reference. We press to no avail upon the springs of our elaborate, miraculous apparatus for cognising the external world: senses, understanding, reason—all go lame. Vainly we hold up the principles found within ourselves, in self-consciousness—will and mind—as a mirror towards the mysterious, invisible essence on the opposing elevation of the divide, and we hope that essence will reveal itself in those principles: yet they reflect no image. But now we also have the right to give this essence that familiar name which from time immemorial has designated what no imaginative power, no flight of the boldest fancy, no thinking however deep or abstract, no composed, devout temperament, no ecstatic mind rapt on high has ever attained: *God*.

But this simple unity *was*; it *is* no more. It has fragmented itself, changing its essence entirely and completely into a world of multiplicity. *God has died and His death was the life of the world.*

Herein lie for the sober-minded thinker two truths which deeply gratify the mind and uplift the heart. We have firstly a *pure, immanent* domain, in or behind or above which no force resides (call it what one will) which has the individuals do now this, now that, like the concealed puppeteer his puppets. We are then uplifted by the truth that everything which now is existed *prior to* the world *in God*. We existed in Him, we can use no other word. If we wanted to say: we lived and moved in Him, then this would be false, for we would be transferring activities of the things of this world onto an essence which was totally inactive and motionless.

Furthermore, *we are no longer in God*; for the simple unity is dead and destroyed. On the contrary, we are in a world of multiplicity, whose individuals are compounded into a solid collective unity.

From the primordial unity we have already derived in the most unforced manner the dynamic coherence of the universe. In the same way we now derive from it the *purposiveness* in the world, which no reasonable person will deny. We remain standing before the disintegration of the unity into multiplicity, without now brooding over why and how this disintegration was accomplished. The fact itself is enough. The disintegration was the deed of a simple unity, its *first* and *last*, its *sole* deed. Every will now existing acquired its essence and motion in this single deed, and for this reason everything in the world encroaches on everything else: the world has a thoroughly purposive constitution.

Finally, we derive indirectly from the primordial unity and directly from the first motion the developmental course of the universe. The disintegration into multiplicity was the first motion, and all motions that followed it—however far they may separate, intertwine, seem to become entangled and in turn disentangled—are only its continuation. The *one* motion of the world, which results *continually* from the actions of all dynamically cohering individuals, is the *fate of the universe*.

God therefore became the world, whose individuals pervasively interact. Since, however, the dynamic coherence consists in the fact that every individual will has an effect on the whole and experiences the efficacy of the whole, but efficacy is motion, so *fate* is nothing other than the *becoming* of the world, the motion of the Orphic conjuncture, the resultant of all individual motions.

I here conclude the Physics by repeating the observation that it is the first attempt to explain nature with inner and outer experience, with the individual will-to-life *alone* (without the aid of any suprasensory force). In saying this it is at the same time likely that in some places I was too timid and have overlooked important details.

One ought also to be mindful of what it means to be the master of all disciplines, the present state of natural science being what it is. The burden of the empirical material is downright oppressive, and only with the magic wand of a clear, irrefutable philosophical principle can the sifting in some way be accomplished, like the chaotic masses of stone which arranged themselves into symmetrical structures according to the sounds of the Orphic lyre.

Such an irrefutable principle is *the individual will-to-life*. I press it like a gift into the hands of every true and honest investigator of nature, wishing that it yield for him better explanations of the phenomena in his delimited field than he has heretofore arrived at. In general, however, I hope that this principle opens up a new path to science on which it is as successful as it was on that one which Bacon opened up to it by means of his inductive method.

I further consider the *pure, immanent* domain, totally freed from the spectre of transcendent essentialities, to be a second gift that I am making to the investigators of nature. How peacefully they shall be able to work in that domain!

I foresee (and I may say this, because the end result of my philosophy is the sole light which imbues my eyes and in them holds my entire will enchained): The complete separation of the immanent from the transcendent domain, the separation of God from the world and of the world from God will have the most beneficial influence on the course of humanity's development. This separation was to be effected only on the basis of genuine transcendental idealism; the correct cut through the ideal and real had to be made first.

I see the dawn of a beautiful day.

♦

Already in the Analytics, pursuing the developmental chains of things-in-themselves (with the aid of time) a parte ante, we found a simple, premundane unity, before which our cognitive faculty went lame. According to the individual faculties of cognition, we defined that unity negatively as: inactive, unextended, undifferentiated, unfragmented, motionless, timeless. We then placed ourselves before this unity once again in the Physics, hoping to catch a glance of it in the mirror of those principles of will and mind which we had found in the meantime, but there too our efforts were completely unsuccessful: *nothing* revealed itself in our mirror. Here too we had therefore to define things once again only negatively, as a simple unity at rest and free, which was neither will nor mind, nor an interpenetration of will and mind.

On the other hand, we obtained three extraordinarily important *positive* results. We recognised that this simple unity, God, fragmenting itself into a world, disappeared entirely and perished; further, that the world which arose from God, precisely because it originated in a simple unity, stands without exception in a dynamic coherence and, in connection with this, that the motion creating itself continuously from the efficacy of all individual beings is fate; finally, that the premundane unity *existed*.

Existence was the thin thread which bridged the chasm between the immanent and transcendent domains, and to existence we have first to turn our attention.

The simple unity existed, we can predicate of it no more than this. Of what type this existence, this being was, is veiled from us entirely. If we want nevertheless to define it more closely, then we must again take refuge in negation and state that it bears no resemblance to any kind of being with which we are familiar, for all being with which we are familiar is *moved* being, is a *becoming*, whereas the simple unity was motionless, in absolute rest. Its being was *supra-being*.

Our positive recognition that the simple unity existed remains entirely untouched by this fact; for the negation does not affect existence as such, but only the kind of existence, a kind which we cannot make comprehensible to ourselves.

Now, from this positive recognition that the simple unity existed flows of its own accord that other, very important realisation that the simple unity also had to have a particular *essence*, for every existentia posits an essentia, and it is simply inconceivable that a premundane unity existed but was in itself without an essence, i.e., that it was nothingness.

But of the essence, the essentia of God, as of His existentia, we can also form for ourselves not the slightest notion. Everything which we apprehend and cognise *in* the world as the essence of individual things is inseparably connected with motion, and God was at rest. If, however, we want to define His essence, then this can only be done negatively, and we must state that the essence of God was an incomprehensible, but in itself quite *definite supra-essence*.

Even our positive recognition that the simple unity had a definite essence remains entirely untouched by this negation.

Thus far everything is clear. But it also seems as if human wisdom had here reached an end and the disintegration of the unity into multiplicity were quite simply unfathomable.

But we are not yet entirely helpless. We have precisely the disintegration of the unity into multiplicity, the transition of the transcendent into the immanent domain, God's death and the birth of the world. We are confronted with a *deed*, the first and sole deed of the simple unity. The immanent domain *followed* on the transcendent, something has become which previously was not. Should it not be possible here to fathom the deed itself, without becoming fantastical and wandering off into wretched hallucinations? We want to be very careful indeed.

We are nevertheless confronted with a process which we can conceive of in no other way than as a deed; we are also thoroughly justified in calling that same process a deed, for we are still standing entirely in the immanent domain, which is nothing other than this very deed.

If, however, we ask after the *factors* which brought this deed about, then we leave the immanent domain and find ourselves on the "shoreless ocean" of the transcendent, which is forbidden us, forbidden because all of our faculties of cognition go lame in that domain.

In the immanent domain, *in* the world, the factors (in themselves) of one deed or another are always known to us. We have constantly on one hand an individual will of an entirely definite character and on the other hand a sufficient motive. Now, if we wanted to use this unshakeable fact in addressing the present question, then we would simply have to describe the world as a deed which sprang from a divine *will* and a divine *intelligence*, i.e., we would be placing ourselves in complete contradiction with the results of immanent philosophy; for we have found that the simple unity was neither will, nor mind, nor an interpenetration of will and mind; or, in Kant's words, we would in the most arbitrary and sophistical manner be making immanent principles into *constitutive* principles in the transcendent domain, which is toto genere different from the immanent.

But here all of a sudden there is opened to us a way out, which we may take without reservation.

We are confronted, as I have mentioned, with a *deed* of the simple unity. If we wanted to call this deed of deeds, as we call all the deeds known to us in the world, a *motivated act of will*, then we would become unfaithful to our vocation, betray the truth, and be simplistic dreamers; for we may attribute to God neither will nor mind. The immanent principles, will and mind, cannot at all be transferred onto the premundane essence, we are not allowed to make them into *constitutive* principles for the *derivation* of the deed.

In contrast, we may make these same immanent principles into *regulative* principles for "the mere *judgement*" of the deed, i.e., we may attempt to explain the arising of the world by conceiving it *as if* it had been a motivated act of will.

The Philosophy of Redemption

The difference is patent.

In the latter case we merely make a problematic judgement, by analogy with the deeds in this world, without madly presuming to render any kind of apodictic judgement about God's essence. In the former case, in contrast, it is claimed without the slightest hesitation that the essence of God, like that of man, was an inextricable compound of will and mind. Whether one says this or expresses oneself more vaguely and calls the will of God potentia-will, resting, inactive will, and the mind of God potentia-mind, resting, inactive mind—one is always striking the results of honest inquiry in the face: for *will* implies *motion* and mind is a part of the will which has precipitated out and has a particular motion. A resting will is a contradictio in adjecto and bears the mark of logical contradiction.

Accordingly, we set foot upon no forbidden path if we conceive God's deed *as if* it had been a motivated act of will and thus, merely for judging the deed, *temporarily* ascribe will and mind to His essence.

That we must ascribe to it will *and* mind and not will alone is clear, for God was in absolute solitude, and nothing existed besides Him. He was unable to be motivated from *without*, but only by means of Himself. In His self-consciousness were mirrored His essence and its existence, nothing more.

It follows from this with logical compulsion that God was able to exercise his freedom (the liberum arbitrium indifferentiae) in only a *single* choice, namely: either to *remain* as He was or *not to be*. To be sure, He also had the freedom *to be other* than he was; but in all directions of this being-other, freedom had to remain latent, because we can conceive no more complete and better being than that of a simple unity.

Thus, only one deed was possible for God, and specifically one *free* deed, because He was subject to no compulsion whatever, because He was able to forgo that deed as well as carry it out, namely, to enter *absolute nothingness*, the nihil negativum, *i.e.*, to annihilate Himself completely, to cease to exist.

Now, if this was His only possible deed and we, in contrast, face an entirely different deed, the *world*, whose being is a constant becoming, then the question throws itself at us: Why did God, if He

Synkrētic

wanted not to be, not crumble into nothingness *directly*? You all must ascribe omnipotence to God, for nothing constrained His power; consequently, if He wanted not to be, then He had also to be annihilated straightaway. But instead there arose a world of multiplicity, a world of struggle. This is an obvious contradiction. How do you all propose to solve it?

The response to this is firstly: It is on one hand certainly established logically that only a single deed was possible for the simple unity: to annihilate itself completely; on the other hand, the world proves that this deed did not occur. But this contradiction can only be an apparent one. Both deeds—the only one logically possible and the actual one—must at root be capable of unification. But how?

It is clear that they can only be unified if it can be proven that God's direct annihilation was impossible due to some *obstacle* or other.

We have therefore to search for this obstacle.

In the question above it was remarked: "You all must ascribe omnipotence to God, for nothing constrained His power." This sentence, however, is false in its generality. God existed alone, in absolute solitude, and it is consequently correct that He was not constrained by anything outside Him; His power was therefore an omnipotence in the sense that nothing lying *outside* Him constrained it. But it was no omnipotence with respect to His *own* power, or in other words, His power was not to be annihilated by itself, the simple unity was unable, by means of itself, to cease to exist.

God had the freedom to *be* as He wanted, but He was not free of His own particular *essence*. God had the omnipotence to carry out His will to *be* some way or other; but He did not have the power *not* to be all at once.

The simple unity had the power to be, in some way or other, other than it was, but it did not have the power suddenly not to be at all. In the former case it remained in *being*, in the latter case it was supposed *not* to be; in this latter case, however, it stood in its own way; for even if we cannot fathom God's essence, we do at least know *that* it was a particular supra-essence, and that this particular supra-essence, reposing in a particular supra-being, was, as a simple unity, not by means of itself able not to be. This was the obstacle.

Theologians of every age have unreservedly predicated omnipotence of God, *i.e.*, they attributed to Him the power to carry out His every will. In doing this, however, none of those theologians thought of the possibility that God can also will Himself to become nothingness. No one has ever considered this possibility. But if one considers it seriously, then one sees that in this *single* case God's omnipotence was constrained by nothing other than itself, that it was no omnipotence in relation to itself.

According to this view, God's one deed, the disintegration into multiplicity, presents itself as the *carrying out* of the logical deed, of the *resolution* not to be, or in other words: The world is the *means* to the *end* of non-being, and specifically the world is the *sole means possible* to that end. God recognised that only by means of the *becoming* of a real world of multiplicity, only by means of the immanent domain, by means of the world, would He be able to convert from *supra-being* to *non-being*.

Incidentally, were it not clear that God's essence was the obstacle to His dissolution into nothingness, then our ignorance of the obstacle would be no cause for concern. We would then simply have to postulate an uncognisable obstacle in the transcendent domain; for in what follows we shall, in the purely immanent domain and leaving no room to doubt, obtain the result that the *universe* is in fact moving out of being into non-being.

The questions which one could here raise, namely, why God did not want non-being *sooner*, and why He preferred non-being to supra-being at all, are devoid of all meaning; for as to the first question, "sooner" is a temporal concept, which in the context of eternity lacks all sense, and as to the second, it is adequately answered by the *fact of the world*. Non-being must simply have earned preference over supra-being, or else God in his perfect wisdom would not have chosen it. And this all the more when one considers the torments experienced by the higher ideas familiar to us, by the animals nearest to us and by men, torments with which alone non-being can be purchased.

Synkrētic

We have only provisionally attributed will and mind to God's essence and conceived God's deed *as if* it had been a motivated act of will in order to gain a regulative principle for the mere judgement of the deed. By this route we also arrived at our objective, and speculative reason may rest content.

However, we are not allowed to leave our idiosyncratic standpoint between the immanent and transcendent domains (we are hanging from the thin thread of existence over the bottomless abyss separating both domains) in order to set foot once more in the firm world, on the sure ground of experience, until we have *declared loudly* once again that God's essence is neither a compound of will and mind, like man's, nor was it an interpenetration of will and mind. The world's true origin will therefore *never* be fathomed by a human mind. All that one can and may do—a warrant of which we too have made use—is infer the divine act through analogy with deeds in the world, but always keeping in mind and never losing sight of the fact that:

> we see through a glass, darkly (1 Cor 13);

and that, according to our limited endowments, we concoct piecemeal an act which, as the unitary act of a simple unity, can *never* be apprehended by a human mind.

Yet the result of this piecemeal composition is satisfactory. Let us also not forget that we could be equally satisfied if the ability to see the divine act through a glass darkly were denied us; for the transcendent domain and its simple unity have vanished without a trace in our world, in which only individual wills exist and beside or behind which nothing more exists, just as *before* the world *only* the simple unity existed. And this world is so rich, it responds so distinctly and clearly to an honest interrogation that the sober-minded thinker turns with a light heart away from the "shoreless ocean" and devotes all his mental power to the divine act, to the book of nature, which lies at all times open before him.

Before we proceed, we want to summarise these results:

    1) God wanted not to be;

2) His essence was the obstacle to His instant entry into non-being;
3) this essence had to disintegrate into a world of multiplicity whose individual essences all strive for non-being;
4) in this striving they impede each other mutually, they struggle with each other and in this way *weaken* their force;
5) God's whole essence passed into the world in a modified form, as a particular sum of force;
6) the whole world, the universe, has *one* objective: non-being, and achieves it through continuous weakening of its sum of force;
7) every individual, through weakening of its force, will be brought to a point in its developmental course where its striving for annihilation can be fulfilled.

Everything which now *is*, once *was* in the simple premundane unity. Therefore, everything which *is*, figuratively speaking, took part in God's resolution not to be, resolved *in him* to convert into non-being. The retarding element, the essence of God, made the instant carrying-out of this resolution impossible. The world, the process in which this retarding element is *gradually eliminated*, had to arise. This process, the general fate of the universe, was determined by the divine wisdom (we speak always figuratively), and *in this divine wisdom* everything which *is* determined its own *individual life-course*.

Now Buddha is correct: Everything that affects me, all the blows and blessings of chance, are *my work—I willed* them. But I do not bring them about with gradual, uncognisable force *in* the world; rather, *prior to* the world, *in* the simple unity, I determined that they should affect me.

Now pantheism too is correct: The *fate of the world* is a unitary one, is the motion of the entire world towards *one* goal; but no simple unity *in* the world carries out this motion, having an effect in *apparent* individuals now in this, now in that direction; rather, a simple unity *prior to* the world determined the entire process, and *in* the world *only real individuals* carry out this process.

Synkrētic

And now Plato too is correct, who in the *Republic* lets each man, before he enters life, choose for himself his own fate, but he does not choose it *immediately prior to birth*; rather, *prior to* the world in general, in the transcendent domain, when the immanent domain still was not, each man himself determined his own lot.

Finally, *freedom* is now united with *necessity*. The world is the *free* act of a *pre*mundane unity; *in* the world, however, there reigns only necessity, because otherwise the goal could *never* be reached. Everything is interlinked of necessity; everything conspires toward a single goal.

And every action of the individual (not only of man, but of *all* ideas in the world) is at once *free* and *necessary*: free, because it was resolved upon *prior to* the world *in* a free unity; necessary, because the resolution is being realised, is becoming a deed *in* the world.

♦

Man has the natural tendency to personify fate and to apprehend absolute nothingness, which stares at him from every grave, as a place of eternal peace, as a *city of peace*, *Nirvana*—as a new Jerusalem:

And God shall wipe away all tears from their eyes; and there shall be no more death, neither sorrow, nor crying, neither shall there be any more pain: for the former things are passed away. (Rev, 21: 4)

It cannot be denied that the notion of a personal, loving Father-God takes deeper hold of the human heart, "the defiant and despondent thing", than abstract fate, and that the notion of a kingdom of heaven where beatified individuals without wants rest blissful in eternal contemplation awakens a more powerful yearning than absolute nothingness. Here, too, immanent philosophy is also mild and benevolent. The principal concern remains that man has overcome the world through *scientific knowledge*. Whether he leaves the cognised fate as it is or whether he gives it once again the lineaments of a loyal father; whether he leaves the cognised objective of the world standing as absolute nothingness or whether he transforms it into a garden of eternal peace bathed in light—this is completely beside the point. Who would want to interrupt this innocent, harmless game of the fancy?

> A fiction that gladdens me,
> Is worth a truth that saddens me.
> **Wieland**

The wise man, however, looks *absolute nothingness* firmly and joyfully in the eye.

The religion of Islam*

Maulana Muhammad Ali†

The very first point to be noted in a discussion on the religion of Islam‡ is that the name of the system is not Muhammadanism, as is generally supposed in the West, but Islam. Muhammad was the name of the Holy Prophet through whom that religion was revealed, and Western writers call it Muhammadanism after him, on the analogy of such names as Christianity, Buddhism, Confucianism and the like, but the name Muhammadanism was absolutely unknown to the followers of that religion to which it has been given by the Western writers, and is not to be found either in the Holy

---

* This extract from *The Religion of Islam: A comprehensive discussion of the sources, principles and practices of Islam* (1936) reproduces the introduction (including footnotes) to that work. Numerical references in brackets are to the Qur'an by *sura* (chapter) and verse. Thus (22:78) refers to *sura* 22, verse 78. Literal references are to reference works and Quranic authorities: (R.) = *Al-Mufridāt fi Gharībi-l-Qur'an*, of Imām Abu-l-Qāsim al-Husain ibn Abu-l-Fadzl al-Rāghib; (LL.) = Lane's *Arabic-English Lexicon*.

† Maulana Muhammad Ali (1874–1951) was a British Indian and Pakistani writer and scholar. He held a Master of Arts in English and lived in Lahore, Pakistan.

‡ The Arabic word for *religion* is *dīn* or *milla*, the root-meaning of the former being *obedience* and *requital*, and that of the latter *to dictate*. *Milla* has special reference to the prophet through whom the religion is revealed, and *dīn* to the individual who follows it (R.). Another word for religion is *madhhab* which is not used in the Holy Qur'an. It is derived from the root *dhahaba* meaning *he went*, and *madhhab* signifies *a way that one pursues in respect of doctrines and practices* in religion, or *an opinion respecting religion* (LL.). According to some authorities, the distinction between the three words is thus expressed: *dīn* in relation to God Who reveals it, *milla* in relation to the prophet through whom it is revealed, and *madhhab* in relation to the *mujtahid* who expounds it. The word *madhhab* as used in Urdu or Persian carries, however, the wider significance of religion.

The religion of Islam

Qur'an or in the sayings of the Holy Prophet. The name of the system as clearly stated in the Holy Qur'an is Islam,* and the name given to those who follow that system is Muslim.† So far from the system being named after its founder, the founder is himself called a Muslim.‡ In fact, every prophet of God is spoken of in the Holy Qur'an as being a Muslim,§ thus showing that Islam is the true religion for the whole of humanity, the various prophets being the preachers of that religion among different nations in different times and the Holy Prophet Muhammad its last and most perfect exponent.

Among the great religions of the world Islam enjoys the distinction of bearing a significant name, a name that points to its very essence. The root-meaning of the word *Islam* is *to enter into peace*,** and a *Muslim* is *one who makes his peace with God and man*. Peace with God implies complete submission to His will, and peace with man is not only to refrain from evil or injury to another but also to do good to him; and both these ideas find expression in the Holy Qur'an itself as the true essence of the religion of Islam: 'Yea, whoever submits (*aslama*) himself entirely to Allah and he is the doer of good to others, he has his reward from his Lord, and there is no fear for such, nor shall they grieve' (2:112). Islam is thus, in its very inception, the religion of peace, and its two basic doctrines, the unity of God and the unity or brotherhood of the human race, afford positive proof of its being true to its name. Not only is Islam

---

* 'This day have I perfected for you your religion and completed My favour on you, and chosen for you Islam as a religion' (5:3). 'Surely the true religion with Allah is Islam' (3:18).

† 'He named you Muslims before and in this' (22:78), where *before* refers to the prophecies, and *this* to the Holy Qur'an.

‡ 'And I am the first of the Muslims' (6:164).

§ 'And the same did Abraham enjoin on his sons and so did Jacob: O my sons! Allah has chosen the religion for you, therefore, die not unless you are Muslims' (2:132); 'We revealed the Torah, in which was guidance and light; with it the prophets who submitted themselves (*aslamū*) judged matters for those who were Jews' (5:44).

** Islam means *entering into salm*, and *salm* and *silm* both signify *peace* (R.). Both these words are used in the sense of *peace* in the Holy Qur'an itself, see 2:208 and 8:61.

Synkrētic

stated to be the true religion of all the prophets of God, as pointed out above, but even the involuntary but complete submission to Divine laws which is witnessed in nature, is indicated by the same word *aslama*. This wider significance is also retained in the strictly legal usage of the word, for, in law, Islam has a two-fold significance; a simple profession of faith—a declaration that there is nothing that deserves to be worshipped but God and that Muhammad is the Messenger of God, and a complete submission to the Divine will which is only attainable through spiritual perfection.[*] Thus, the man who simply accepts the religion of Islam, the mere novice, is a Muslim, as well as he who completely submits himself to the Divine will and carries out in practice all the Divine commandments, subduing his desires to the will of God.

Islam is the last of the great religions—those mighty movements which have revolutionised the world and changed the destinies of nations. But it is not only the last religion, it is an all-inclusive religion which contains within itself all religions which went before it, and one of its most striking characteristics is that it requires its followers to believe that all the great religions of the world that preceded it have been revealed by God. It is a fundamental principle of Islam that a Muslim must also believe in all the prophets who were raised up before the Holy Prophet Muhammad:

'And who believe in that which has been revealed to thee and that which was revealed before thee' (2:4).

'Say: We believe in Allah and in that which has been revealed to us and in that which was revealed to Abraham and Ishmael and Isaac and Jacob and the tribes, and in that which was given to Moses and Jesus and in that which was given to the prophets from their Lord; we do not make any distinction between any of them' (2:136).

---

[*] 'Islam in law is of two kinds; one is a simple confession with the tongue . . . whether accompanied with belief (*īmān* or *real change*) in the heart or not. . . . The other is above belief (*īmān*), and it means that along with confession, there is belief (*īmān* or *real change*) in the heart and a fulfilment in practice, and resignation to God in whatever He brings to pass or decrees' (R.).

'The Apostle believes in what has been revealed to him from his Lord, and so do the believers; they all believe in Allah and His angels and His books and His apostles; we make no difference between any of His apostles' (2:285).

Thus a Muslim believes not only in the Prophet Muhammad but in all other prophets as well. And prophets were, according to the express teachings of the Holy Qur'an, raised up among all the nations: 'And there is not a nation but a warner has gone among them' (35:24). A Muslim, therefore, is one who believes in the prophets and scriptures of all the nations. A Jew believes only in the prophets of Israel; a Christian believes in Jesus Christ and, in a lesser degree, in the prophets of Israel; a Buddhist in Buddha; a Zoroastrian in Zoroaster; a Hindu in the prophets raised up in India; a Confucian in Confucius; but a Muslim believes in all these and in Muhammad also, the last of the prophets. Islam is, therefore, an all-comprehensive religion within which are included all the religions of the world; and, similarly, its sacred Book, the Holy Qur'an, is spoken of as a combination of all the sacred scriptures of the world: 'Pure pages wherein are all the right scriptures' (98:2,3).

There is yet one more characteristic of Islam which gives it a special place among religions. In addition to being the last religion of the world and an all-inclusive religion, it is the perfect expression of the Divine will. Thus the Holy Qur'an: 'This day have I perfected for you your religion and completed My favour on you, and chosen for you Islam as a religion' (5:3). Like every other form of consciousness, the religious consciousness of man has developed slowly and gradually down the ages, and the revelation of the great Truth from on high was thus brought to perfection in Islam. It is to this great truth that the words of Jesus Christ allude: 'I have yet many things to say unto you but ye cannot bear them now. Howbeit when he, the spirit of truth, is come, he will guide you into all truth' (John 16:12,13). Thus it is the great mission of Islam to bring about peace in the world by establishing a brotherhood of all the religions of the world, to gather together all the religious truths contained in previous religions, to correct their errors and to sift the true from the false, to preach the eternal verities which had not before been preached on account of the special circumstances of any race or society in the early stages of its development, and last of all to meet all the moral and spiritual requirements of an ever-advancing humanity.

With the advent of Islam, religion has received new significance. Firstly it is to be treated not as a dogma, which a man must accept if he will escape everlasting damnation, but as a science based on the universal experience of humanity. It is not this or that nation that becomes the favourite of God and the recipient of Divine revelation; on the contrary revelation is recognised as a necessary factor in the evolution of man; hence while in its crudest form it is the universal experience of humanity, in its highest, that of prophetical revelation, it has been a Divine gift bestowed upon all nations of the world. And the idea of the scientific in religion has been further strengthened by presenting its doctrines as principles of actions. There is not a single doctrine of religion which is not made the basis of action for the development of man to higher and yet higher stages of life. Secondly, the sphere of religion is not confined to the next world; its primary concern is rather with this life, and that man, through a righteous life here on earth, may attain to the consciousness of a higher existence. And so it is that the Holy Qur'an deals with a vast variety of subjects which affect man's life below. It deals not only with the ways of devotion, with the forms of worship of the Divine Being, with the means which make man attain communion with God, but also, and in richer detail, with the problems of the world around us, questions of relations between man and man, his social and political life, institutions of marriage, divorce and inheritance, the division of wealth and the relations of labour and capital, the administration of justice, military organisation, peace and war, national finance, debts and contracts, rules for the service of humanity and even of dumb creation, laws for the help of the poor, the orphan and the widow, and hundreds of other questions the proper understanding of which enables man to lead a happy life. It lays down rules not only for individual progress but also for the advancement of society as a whole, of the nation and even of humanity. It casts a flood of light on problems relating to relations not only between individuals but also between the different tribes and nations into which humanity is divided. And all these rules and laws are made effective by a faith in God. It prepares man for another life, it is true, but only through making him capable of holding his own in this.

The question which perturbs every mind today is whether religion is, when all is said and done, necessary to humanity.

Now a cursory glance at the history of human civilisation will show that religion has been the supreme force in the development of mankind to its present condition. That all that is good and noble in man has been inspired by faith in God is a truth at which perhaps even an atheist would not cavil. One Abraham, one Moses, one Christ, one Krishna, one Buddha, one Muhammad has, each in his turn and his degree, changed the whole history of the human race and raised it from the depths of degradation to moral heights undreamed of. It is through the teachings of this or that great prophet that man has been able to conquer his lower nature and to set before himself the noblest ideals of selflessness and the service of humanity. Study the noble sentiments that inspire man today and you will find their origin in the teachings and example of some great sage who had a deep faith in God and through whom was sown the seed of faith in other human hearts. The moral and ethical development of man to his present state, if due to any one cause, is due to religion. Humanity has yet to find out whether the lofty emotions which inspire man today will survive after a generation or two of godlessness, and what sentiments materialism will bring in its train. To all appearance, the reign of materialism must needs entail the rule of selfishness; for a cut and dried scheme for the equal division of wealth will not inspire the noble sentiments which are today the pride of man and which centuries of religion have instilled into his very being. If the sanction of religion be removed today, the ignorant masses—and the masses must always remain ignorant though they may be able to read and write a little—will sink back, gradually of course, into a state of savagery, while even those who reckon themselves above the common level will no longer feel the inspiration to noble and high ideals which only faith in God can give.

Synkrētic

    As a matter of fact, human civilisation, as we have it today, is, whether it likes the idea or not, based on religion. Religion has made possible a state of civilisation which has again and again saved human society from disruption. Trace back its history in all nations, and it will be seen that whenever it has begun to totter, a new religious impulse has always been at hand to save it from utter destruction. It is not only that civilisation, with any pretence to endurance, can rest only on a moral basis, and that true and lofty morals are inspired only by faith in God, but even the unity and cohesion of jarring human elements, without which it is impossible for any civilisation to stand for a day, is best brought about by the unifying force of religion. It is often said that religion is responsible for much of the hatred and bloodshed in the world, but a cursory glance at the history of religion will show this to be a monstrous misconception. Love, concord, sympathy, kindness to one's fellow-men, have been the message of every religion, and every nation has learnt these essential lessons in their true purity only through the spirit of selflessness and service which a faith in God has inspired. If there have been selfishness and hatred and bloodshed, they have been there in spite of religion, not as a consequence of the message of love which religion has brought. They have been there because human nature is too prone to these things; and their presence only shows that a still greater religious awakening is required, that a truer faith in God is yet a crying need of humanity. That men shall sometimes turn to low and unworthy things does not show that the nobler sentiments are worthless but only that their development has become a more urgent necessity.

    If unification be the true basis of human civilisation, by which phrase I mean the civilisation not of one nation or of one country but of humanity as a whole, then Islam is undoubtedly the greatest civilizing force the world has ever known or is likely to know. Thirteen hundred years ago it was Islam that saved it from crushing into an abyss of savagery, that came to the help of a civilisation whose very foundations had collapsed, and that set about laying new foundation and rearing an entirely new edifice of culture and ethics. A new idea of the unity of the human race as a whole, not of the unity of this or that nation, was introduced into the world, an idea so mighty that it welded together nations which had warred with and hated each other since the world began. It was not only in Arabia, among the ever-bickering tribes of a single peninsula, that this great 'miracle', as an English writer terms it, was wrought,* a miracle before the magnitude of which every thing dwindles into insignificance. It not only cemented together the warring tribes of one country but it established a brotherhood of all nations of the world, even joining together those which had nothing in common except their common humanity. It obliterated differences of colour, race, language, geographical boundaries and even differences of culture. It united man with man as such, and the hearts of those in the far east began to beat in unison with the hearts of those in the farthest west. Indeed, it proved to be not only the greatest but the only force unifying man, because, whereas other religions had succeeded merely in unifying the different elements of a single race, Islam had actually achieved the unification of many races, had harmonised the jarring and discordant elements of humanity. How great a force it was in bringing back his lost civilisation to man, is attested by a recent writer:†

'In the fifth and sixth centuries, the civilized world stood on the verge of chaos. The old emotional cultures that had made civilization possible, since they had given to men a sense of unity and of reverence for their rulers, had broken down, and nothing had been found adequate to take their place . . .

'It seemed then that the great civilization which it had taken four thousand years to construct was on the verge of disintegration, and that mankind was likely to return to that condition of barbarism where every tribe and sect was against the next and law and order were unknown. . . . The old tribal sanctions had lost their power. . . .

---

* 'A more disunited people it would be hard to find till suddenly the miracle took place. A man arose who, by his personality and by his claim to direct Divine guidance, actually brought about the impossible—namely the union of all those warring factions' (*The Ins and Outs of Mesopotamia*, p. 99).

† *Emotion as the Basis of Civilization*, by J. H. Denison.

Synkrētic

The new sanctions created by Christianity were working division and destruction instead of unity and order. . . . Civilization like a gigantic tree whose foliage had over-reached the world . . . stood tottering . . . rotted to the core. . . . Was there any emotional culture that could be brought in to gather mankind once more into unity and to save civilization?' (pp. 265—268).

And then speaking of Arabia, the learned author says:

'It was among these people that the man was born who was to unite the whole known world of the east and south' (p. 269).

Thus Islam laid the basis of a unification of humanity of which no other reformer or religion has ever dreamed; of a brotherhood of man which knows no bounds of colour, race, country, language or even of rank; of a unity of the human race beyond which human conception cannot go. It not only recognises the equality of the civil and political rights of men, but also that of their spiritual rights. 'All men are a single nation' (2:213) is its fundamental doctrine, and for that reason every nation is recognised as having received the spiritual gift of revelation. But the establishment of a vast brotherhood of all men is not its only achievement. Equally great is the unparalleled transformation which Islam has brought about in the world; for Islam has proved itself to be a spiritual force the equal of which the human race has never known. Its miraculous transformation of world conditions was brought about in an incredibly short space of time. It swept away the vilest superstitions, the crassest ignorance, the rank immorality, the old evil habits of centuries over centuries, in less than a quarter of a century. That its spiritual conquests are without parallel in history is an undeniable fact, and it is because of the unparalleled spiritual transformation effected by him that the Holy Prophet Muhammad is admitted to be the 'most successful of all prophets and religious personalities' (En. Br., art. Koran).

Islam has a claim upon the attention of every thinker, not only because it is the most civilising and the greatest spiritual force of the world but also because it offers a solution of the most baffling problems which confront mankind today. Materialism, which has become humanity's ideal in modern times, can never bring about peace and mutual trust among the nations of the world. Christianity has already failed to do away with race and colour prejudices. Islam is the only force which has already succeeded in blotting out those distinctions and it is through Islam only that this great problem of the modern world can be solved. Islam is, first and foremost, an international religion, and it is only before the grand international ideal of Islam, the ideal of the equality of all races and of the unity of the human race, that the curse of nationalism which has been and is responsible for the troubles of the ancient and the modern worlds, can be swept away. But even within the boundaries of a nation or a country there can be no peace so long as a just solution of the two great problems of wealth and sex be not found. Europe has gone to two extremes on the wealth question, capitalism and Bolshevism. There is either the tendency to concentrate wealth among the great capitalists or by community of wealth to bring the indolent and the industrious to one level. Islam offers the true solution by ensuring to the worker the reward of his work, great or small, in accordance with the merit of the work, and also by allotting to the poor a share in the wealth of the rich. Thus while the rights of property are maintained in their fullest sense, an arrangement is made for equalising conditions by taking a part of the wealth of the rich and distributing it among the poor according to the principle of *zakāt*, and also by a more or less equal division of property among heirs on the death of an owner. Thus H.A.R. Gibb[1] writing towards the close of *Whither Islam* says:

'Within the western world Islam still maintains the balance between exaggerated opposites. Opposed equally to the anarchy of European nationalism and the regimentation of Russian communism, it has not yet succumbed to that obsession with the economic side of life which is characteristic of present-day Europe and present-day Russia alike. Its social ethic has been admirably summed up by Professor Massignon: "Islam has the merit of standing for a very equalitarian conception of the contribution of each citizen by the tithe to the resources of the community; it is hostile to unrestricted exchange, to banking capital, to state loans, to indirect taxes on objects of prime necessity, but it holds to the rights of the father and the husband, to private property, and to commercial capital.

Here again it occupies intermediate position between the doctrines of bourgeois capitalism and Bolshevist communism'" (pp. 378-379).

Similarly Islam's solution of the sex question is the only one that can ensure ultimate peace to the family. There is neither the free-love which would loosen all ties of social relations, nor the indissoluble binding of man and woman which turns many a home into an actual hell. And by solving these and a hundred other problems which puzzle the minds of men today, Islam, as its very name indicates, can bring true happiness to the human race.

The anti-religious movement which has taken root in Russia is based on a misconception as to the nature of the religion of Islam. The three chief objections to religion are:

(1) That religion helps in the maintenance of the present social system which has borne the fruit of capitalism with a consequent crushing of the aspirations of the poor.

(2) That it keeps the people subject to superstition and thus hinders the advance of sciences.

(3) That it teaches them to pray for their needs instead of working for them and thus it makes them indolent.*

So far as Islam is concerned, the facts are entirely contrary to these allegations. Islam came as the friend of the poor and the destitute, and as a matter of fact it has accomplished an upliftment of the poor to which history affords no parallel. It raised men at the lowest rung of the social ladder to the highest positions of life, it made of slaves not only leaders in thought and intellect but actually kings. Its social system is one of an equality which is quite unthinkable in any other nation or any other society. It lays down, as one of the fundamental principles of religion, that the poor have a *right* in the wealth of the rich, a right which is exercised through the state which collects annually a fortieth of the wealth amassed by the rich, to distribute it among the poor.

---

* As summed up in *Emotion as the Basis of Civilization*, p. 506.

As regards the second allegation that religion discourages the advancement of science and learning, this is equally devoid of truth, so far as Islam is concerned. Islam gave an impetus to learning in a country which had never possessed a seat of learning and was sunk in the depths of superstition. Even as far back as the caliphate of 'Umar, the Islamic state undertook the education of the masses, while the Muslims carried the torch of learning to every country where they gained political ascendancy—schools, colleges and universities springing up everywhere as a result of the Muslim conquest—and it is no exaggeration but simple truth to say that it was through Islam that the Renaissance came about in Europe.

The third allegation that religion makes people idle by teaching them to pray is also belied by the history of Islam. Not only does the Holy Qur'an teach men to work their best and hardest for success in life, and lay down, in plain words, that 'man shall have nothing but what he strives for' (53:39), but it actually made the most neglected nation in the world, the Arabs, a nation of supreme conquerors in all phases of life. And this great revolution was brought about only by awakening in them a desire for work and a zest for hard striving. Islam does teach man to pray, no one will dispute that; but prayer instead of making him idle is to fit him for a still harder struggle, and to carry on that struggle in the face of failure and disappointment, by turning to God Who is the Source of all strength. Thus prayer in Islam is only an incentive to work and not a hindrance.

Notes

1 Sir Hamilton Alexander Rosskeen Gibb (1895–1971) was a Scottish historian and Orientalist.

RESPONSES
What is Indian philosophy?

The art of living in harmony

*Aaron Ortner**

You are a PhD candidate at the University of Hawai'i at Mānoa and your background is in ancient philosophy, Greek and Latin. Did these ancient languages bring you to philosophy or was it the other way around?

Like many of us, I think, the embryo of philosophy was nourished by language. I began studying Latin at fifteen because my stepfather was hired by Bolchazy-Carducci Publishers to adapt Waldo Sweet's *Artes Latinae* to a digital format. I was a guinea pig for the project but warmed to Latin because it clarified my thinking and threw my conceptual framework into greater relief. Wittgenstein might say that my concepts became more pronounced. By the time I started studying Greek at twenty-seven, I had already spent years pursuing philosophy. My background with Latin made plain to me that, if I were to make any great advancement with Greek thinkers, grounding myself in their language would be a critical venture.

What is the focus of your thesis?

I intend to explore how the analogical dialectic that forms the foundation of Aristotelian identity transitions into A.N. White-

---

* Aaron Ortner is a PhD candidate at the University of Hawai'i at Mānoa. He holds a Master of Philosophy in the classics, focussing on Ancient Philosophy, Greek, and Latin. He lives in Honolulu, Hawaii, U.S.A.

head's 'actual occasion'. The 'actual occasion' is most generally the analogical relation of space and time that unites them as a continuum and serves as the basis for a form of identity constituting thought and extension that I call 'constels'.

Philosophy in the Western canon begins in Ancient Greece, and yet we know that Indian thought influenced Greek philosophy early on. Pythagoras is said to have travelled to India. How deep were these intellectual currents?

The intellectual currents flowing between the two are far deeper and more complex than any one instance can show. It is quite true that India influenced Greek philosophy on several levels. At the most general level, it seems that there was an infusion of Indian thought into Presocratic Greece and then a dialectical contribution from Greece to India around the second century A.D. There are obvious similarities between the *Iliad* and the *Mahābhārata* and the *Odyssey* and the *Rāmāyaṇa*. The development of the One and Many along with Macrocosm and Microcosm seem to be down to an influence on Pythagoras. Along with this, the level of detail concerning metempsychosis between the Upanishads and Heraclitus provide powerful evidence of Indian influence.

While there is endless debate concerning the precision of date and detail, scholars generally estimate the development of Indian philosophy as being between 1500 and 500 B.C. The Greeks made rapid strides with many similar concepts between 700 to 500 B.C. Such a quick development in Greece, compounded most of all by the demonstration that Heraclitus borrowed from some Upanishads (and the general Persian connection in Ionian politics and therefore its educated class) suggests that Greek philosophy was given some impetus by influences from India through the mediation of the Persian empire and its political assemblage.

What other interesting connections have you found between ancient Indian and Greek thought?

Synkrētic

A sensible view is that some ideas occur independently while others are influenced. Similarity in detail often suggests a broader foundation of similarity, maybe even to the degree by which we may discover a common root. After all, independent ideation seems as likely to occur on an individual scale as on a societal one, or even the entirety of the species. For instance, one may study a text and draw conclusions that have already been contemplated elsewhere. Indeed, our internal power of reason might be likely to generate identical ideas because the external world provides us with similar 'texts' as it were.

The diffusion from India to Heraclitus is indicated when we see similar details or advancements in short periods that have taken much longer elsewhere. Heraclitus' system of five transformations (elemental) and two exhalations (the Greek equivalent of Indian *samsara* and *moksha* in which the soul either returns to another body or is released from the cosmic cycle) are not preceded by similar characterisations before him in the Presocratic traditions, yet the exact same series of transmutations occur throughout Upanishadic literature (Brihadaranyaka, Yajnavalkya, Chandogya, and the Kausltaki Upanishads).

For instance, Heraclitus' 'dark exhalation' recycles the soul back into a reincarnated body by a certain order of transition through the elements, Soul:Water:Earth:Water:Soul. This is called the 'path of the fathers', which eventually proceeds through smoke to a re-entrance of the cosmic wheel of rebirth, while another, the path of the gods, follows a different order and goes through fire to a release from the cosmic wheel to the realm of gods. But these are very particular and exact similarities. This suggests that there ought to be a continuity of tradition that can explain the combinations of a complex system as it has gone through discrete stages of development. This example, then, shows how an influential Greek Presocratic derived his doctrine from India.

On the other hand, India only had a "proto-dialectic" before the Alexandrian diffusion. Much of the same process occurred there. Such a proto-dialectic is indicated in the structure of the Loka yakitas doctrines and the Lokayata schools, Sañjaya, and the Jain doctrine known as the *syādvāda*. Likewise, Nāgārjuna systematised Siddhartha's use of skeptical denials after the Alexandrian diffusion. While India did not have a fully generated dialectical method until Nāgārjuna or later, dialectics itself was a mode of thought derived from *ideas* that diffused from India to Greece during the Presocratic age. The notion of cyclical time, One and Many, Macro and Micro, and the tripartite doctrine of reincarnation. This is because, explicit or not, dialectical modes of thought must have been latent in construing the idea of substrate from the One and the Many, as Plato used dialectic to complete Parmenides' riddles. Pythagoras unites the One and Many through the harmony of numeric ratio. This necessarily leads to the inference of uniting various types of motion, drawing the necessary link between the finite (straight line) microcosmic human and the eternal macrocosmic god (curved or circular).

Dialectical circulation is also the process of diffusion between major and hitherto considered isolated cultures. That means that the circulation of ideas between traditions is part of the structure and shape of each individual tradition so that the common structure of ideation is circular in part and whole. In other words, the dialectical progression of ideas that guides and culminates in any given tradition, say, Greek or Indian philosophy, can also be found within the wider realm of ideational development between societies, like microcosms to their universal macrocosm.

The Precession of Equinoxes might exhibit the root of such a dialectic. It is the foundation of myth, yet no one is able to triangulate the location of its origin. It is likely the foundation of the syncretic nature of myths, religions, and philosophical systems of thought. Most likely it centres on the 2nd millennium B.C. in or around Mesopotamia. Still, its dialectical nature can be seen in the attempt to reconcile the geometry of space and astronomy with the arithmetic of music. Where the former provides objective empirical organisation to the world, the latter introduces the narrative exposition of subjective experience, both of which combine to generate mythic stories in order to create an objective ethical system.

Synkrētic

Indeed, the combination of the sexagesimal (circular) and decimal (straight) systems created numerological foundations for the Platonic Solids in the *Republic* and the genealogies of Genesis. Plato's five solids, for instance, can be derived from certain numbers that are contained in the *Phaedrus* and *Republic* myths. The simplest solids as formed by the triangles under the ratio of the root of two and the root of three, which are combined in the golden ratio Φ (1.68) as a fifth the dodecahedron, which is quite literally Time and the Space of the Fixed Stars, or the motion of the Same (Φ is the symbol of both philosophy and the Golden Ratio, symbolising the combination of the curved, or circle, and the straight.). Geometrically, each of the four solids represents a soul and its analogous state that, when organised symmetrically, form *Kallipolis*, the ideal city.

The point is that, while this progression took over a millennium to reach its full import in Plato, its mythic, astrological character shows clear signs of dialectical progression. Both regions, though bracketed from each other, were able to draw together by realising the same cosmic principles that express themselves in humanity's power structures.

If you have one, who is your favourite ancient Greek thinker and which idea of theirs do you think has burning relevance to debates in contemporary philosophy—or quite simply to modern life?

That is a difficult question because I can't decide between Plato and Aristotle. The full answer to this question, at least for me, can be found in Whitehead's *Science in the Modern World*. There he draws out several themes of relevance here in the form of debunking the fallacies of misplaced concreteness and simple location. Fundamentally, these fallacies are responsible for the 'vacuous actuality' that is at the core of scientific nihilism. These are not only philosophically incoherent but are even morally divisive. Our inability to resolve quantum mechanics and Einsteinian relativity lie in our inability to let go of Cartesian fallacies.

Are you seeing growing interest in ancient Indian philosophy? What are some opportunities and limitations for classical Indian thought to be studied and taught in universities in the West today?

Well, as with anything, when one begins to study an area, one tends to find a new world of emergent interest. The West tends to be complacent in studying any other tradition than its own. I have been guilty of that for too long. ANU and UH Manoa are trailblazing a higher form of dialectical philosophical education. Yet, I do think students should be well-grounded in their own tradition. It makes for a truly greater adventure when one begins to look elsewhere. There is so much in both traditions that I feel it may be an error to attempt taking it all in at once. There should be some sort of balance, I think, but I am not the one to know what that is.

You live and work in Hawaii. *Synkrētic* has a strong focus on the thought and traditions of the wider Indo-Pacific, including the Pacific. Are there connecting points between ancient Greek and Indigenous Pacific thought?

Well, as with my response to the question pertaining to Indian and Greek diffusion, I think that the obvious connection is astronomy and myths. I am no expert in Hawaiian lore, but people such as Bruce Ka'imi Watson are researching and teaching on the subject of Hawaiian philosophy. It is likely that the philosophical tradition of Hawai'i was capsized by the advent of the West. They seemed to be developing something along the lines of epistemology. I look forward to seeing what Ka'imi finds.

You have written a paper in the form of a Platonic dialogue about modern philosophers travelling back in time to Ancient Greece to thrash out philosophical problems.[1] What inspired your fantastic premise?

I was inspired to write the dialogue as an undergraduate who had a fervent belief that the Western tradition had lost its way (much as Whitehead describes it). I was not yet very familiar with American process philosophy or the phenomenologists, otherwise I might have been less severe in criticising modernity for forgetting its roots. That was the point of the time travel aspect, that Western philosophy was dead. Scholars, I thought (and still think true of some circles), had simplified the ancient Greeks in the same manner that Nietzsche and Heidegger criticised academia: they lost sight of analogical dialectic.

Your time travellers Theodore Sider and Derek Parfit, as well as their companions Bernard Williams, John Locke, Plato, and Aristotle, do not come to any agreement on the nature of persistent identity, do they?

No. Theodore Sider and Derek Parfit convey chronological superiority. They think their simplistic notions are greater than ancient ones which serve as the foundations of their own thought.

Plato was not just a great in philosophy but a great storyteller, as were other philosophical writers like Voltaire, Kierkegaard, Dostoyevsky, and Sartre. What part do you think creativity plays in producing good philosophy?

I think creativity is essential to good philosophy. Indeed, I think understanding the past by uniting it with the present is an act of creative 'recollection'. Plato was a playwright who reorganised Homer and Greek drama according to the concepts that were recently emerging. I think every philosopher (and every person in general) would benefit greatly from learning music comprehensively. To understand the 'movement' of the universe means more than physics. It comes through familiarity with creative themes and harmonies. For Whitehead, philosophy and the human intelligence advances by acts of creative novelty that harmonise the universe such that good prevails and reshapes evil. Nietzsche and many existentialists believe that life is justified only as an aesthetic project.

Aristotle suggests in his *Poetics* that ethics can only be fully understood when human action and history are conceived of as on a stage (poetry is more philosophical than history). Intellect, when utilised as a harvester of data, is only half realised. When different forms of data are creatively compared, the categories by which we understand the self and 'the other' arise. When we understand that the feather of a bird is the scale of a fish, we are able to understand Aristotle's Category of 'shod'. They all work like that, which is why Kant's schematism arises from the 'analogies of experience'. To develop a metaphor, Aristotle says, is the greatest form of genius.

For this very reason, I think your journal, *Synkrētic*, is so important. It underscores the importance of not elevating one ideology over another. It understands that thought and philosophy are dialectical. Karl Jaspers thought this was the most important step in reshaping civilisation after World War II. It is the art of living in harmony. I think he is right and that what you are doing is bolstering that effort. Thanks for the interview and good luck!

Notes

1 Aaron Ortner, 'Time Travels to Greece: On Persistent Identity', *Academia.edu*, available at: <https://www.academia.edu/33086710/Time_Travels_to_Greece_On_Persistent_Identity>.

The problem of evil in Hindu thought

*Akshay Gupta**

Your recent article in *Philosophy East and West*[1] discusses the age-old problem of evil in theology. What attracted you to this particular question?

I've been interested in questions related to human suffering since my undergraduate years. As I began to think of a topic to pursue for my doctorate, the topic of suffering was a natural choice. Initially, I was interested in the idea that God causes instances of suffering for God's devotees in order to bring them closer to God—this is an idea found throughout the *Bhagavata Purana*. This naturally led me to focus on the problem of evil and how it has been formulated and advanced in contemporary philosophy.

Which version of the problem are you responding to?

I primarily respond to the evidential problem of evil.

In the Middle Ages, Catholic theologians, among others in different traditions before and after them, developed theodicies to reconcile the existence of suffering with God's existence. How much has the debate in the modern literature moved on from these classical formulations?

---

* Akshay Gupta is Visiting Assistant Professor at the College of William and Mary. He holds a PhD in theology and religious studies from the University of Cambridge. He lives in Williamsburg, Virginia, U.S.A.

To a certain extent, many of the ideas of these theologians are still found in the modern literature. Eleonore Stump wrote a relatively recent book defending Thomas Aquinas' views on the problem of evil for example.[2] Free will continues to play an important role in most current theodicies, and has done for centuries. What's different about the modern literature is how it incorporates many of the tools of analytic philosophy, but you can still see the many intellectual inheritances from earlier times.

One old argument is that God gave people free will, such that evil, especially man-made evil like wars and economic inequalities, are not divinely ordained but are perhaps permitted because we were made free. How does the free will view in the contemporary literature differ from this?

You can still find this view in the literature, but generally there is more of an attempt to identify additional goods that result from evils. One common line of thinking is to say that evils and suffering lead to soul-making and help individuals develop a better moral character. Other responses might say that suffering helps individuals grow closer to God by deepening their devotion to God.

Your article explores Hindu responses to the problem of evil with a focus on the *Bhāgavata Purāṇa*. What should readers know about this text to better understand your argument?

The *Bhāgavata Purāṇa* is one of the most important Hindu sacred texts, and it largely focuses on the deity Krishna, who can plausibly be conceived of as an all-powerful, all-knowing, all-good God.

Also all-powerful, Krishna is the complete sovereign of the world. Is he a God comparable to the God of the Abrahamic religions?

With respect to these divine attributes, I would say yes. There are differences in other areas. For example, Krishna has a divine, spiritual body, whereas God is not considered to be embodied in the Abrahamic traditions.

Synkrētic

What are some of the reasons that such a God would produce suffering in his followers?

One reason is to deepen the devotion of God's devotees. In times of crisis, individuals often pray to God more fervently and sincerely, and on the whole this intensification of devotion is a valuable good in the context of the *Bhāgavata Purāṇa*, as the ultimate aim in this text is for individuals to develop a loving relationship with God, which requires a certain purity to an individual's devotion.

Another reason for suffering is that it can teach individuals certain moral lessons that shape their character. For instance, by experiencing pain, you can develop a greater sensitivity to others by reference to your own pain.

An additional reason for suffering is that it can enable one to develop a dispassionate outlook toward the world. This is important within a Hindu context, because attaining liberation from the world and love for God requires that one devote oneself wholeheartedly to God—and worldly attachments can sometimes impede the development of this devotion.

You mention a story in the *Mahābhārata* that is about forgiving even an act of horrific suffering. Does this mean that even such suffering can be reformative and develop us morally?

Yes, even intense moments of suffering can be reformative—even if not immediately. In a Hindu context, experiences of suffering leave "impressions" that persist in an individual's "subtle body"—a mental body that individuals remain associated with as they reincarnate across various physical bodies. An experience of suffering can leave a strong impression, which can mould an individual's psychology in a beneficial way, even if the effects of this are not immediate. For instance, a painful car crash may give a strong impression of pain. Initially, there may be some trauma, but once this has been processed, an individual may be, for example, more sensitive to the pain of others and more aware of the harsh realities of the world—which is a realisation that can propel them on a path toward God. This formation of moral character can also persist as an individual reincarnates.

We are not always best qualified to measure the real significance of events that may seem evil to us, and which from a God's-eye view may look quite different. What do you think are this argument's implications for ethics?

That is an interesting question. I think that as far as ethics goes, individuals should try to do their best according to what they deem moral (for Hindus, this will involve consulting Hindu scriptural texts on certain issues). While it is true that individuals don't have a full God's-eye picture of everything, it is also true that it is not an individual's duty to try to fulfill God's ultimate plan. All one can do is try one's best and act in accordance with God's will (which, for theists, involves acting ethically according to injunctions of scripture), and God can sort out the rest.

What other texts in the Hindu tradition are or should be read as companions to contemporary debates in the philosophy of religion?

There's not a whole lot of work out yet. There's an exchange on karma in *Philosophy East and West* involving Whitley Kaufman, Monima Chadha, and Nick Trakakis.[3] That's worth checking out. There is an upcoming volume on Vaishnavism, to be published with Routledge and to be edited by Ricardo Silvestre and Alan Herbert. The *International Journal for Hindu Studies* had a recent issue on theodicy as well.[4]

Notes

1 Akshay Gupta, 'The *Bhāgavata Purāṇa* and the Problem of Evil', in *Philosophy East and West*, Vol. 73, No. 1 (2023): 66-81.
2 Eleonore Stump, *Wandering in Darkness: Narrative and the Problem of Suffering* (Oxford: Oxford University Press, 2012).

3   Whitley R. P. Kaufman, 'Karma, Rebirth, and the Problem of Evil', in *Philosophy East and West*, Vol. 55, Issue 1 (2005): 15-32; Monima Chadha and Nick Trakakis, 'Karma and the Problem of Evil: A Response to Kaufman', in *Philosophy East and West*, Vol. 57, No. 4 (October 2007): 533-556.
4   Swami Medhananda (ed.), *International Journal for Hindu Studies*, Vol. 25, Issue 3 (December 2021), Special Issue on Vedantic Theodicies.

The Eastern wisdom of ancient India

*Krishna Pathak**

Professor Pathak, you are the editor of a 2021 collection on mysticism in both East and West.[1] Does this work explore any direct or indirect connections between Hindu and Western philosophical traditions?

Thank you for giving me this wonderful opportunity to discuss my works and philosophical thoughts with *Synkrētic*. Yes, the book does explore the connection. I have a major chapter of my own in this book which is a brief comparative study of the philosophical aspects of both Vedic mysticism and Christian mysticism.[2] A dedicated section of the chapter argues that the source of cosmic origin in the Vedas appears to be ontologically and epistemologically 'more mysterious than God in Christianity'.[3] In fact, one of the main features of the book is that it contains research papers not only on Vedic philosophy and Christian theology, but also on Buddhism, Jainism, Advaitism, ancient Greek philosophy, and medieval and modern European philosophy. So, from the discussion of the book, the readers can definitely draw some sets of direct and indirect parallels between Hindu and Western philosophical traditions. I am pretty sure that the research material and the erudite

---

* Krishna Mani Pathak is Associate Professor of Philosophy at Hindu College, the University of Delhi. He holds a PhD in philosophy from the University of Heidelberg. He lives in New Delhi, India.

inputs of this book will prove to be a very important reference source for any inquisitive mind.

You have been a member of the Kant society and wrote your PhD on the universalisability of Kant's categorical imperative. In your research, have you come across any similarities between Kantian and Hindu ethics?

It is true that I was a member of the Kant Society and even today I am associated with the society in one way or the other. Since the fundamentality of Kant's universalism theory and its indispensability in building an ethical society is similar to the concepts of Niṣkāma Karma and Svadharma given in the Hindu classical scripture the *Srimad Bhagavad Gita*, I realised that a worthwhile justification for writing a PhD would be the topic of 'The Universalizability of the Categorical Imperative: Re-examining Kant's Maxim of Duty', and thankfully I successfully did it. Although the thesis is primarily an analysis of Kant's moral philosophy and a defensive effort in favour of Kant's universalism against the communitarianism and neo-Aristotelianism of the American philosopher Alasdair MacIntyre and the Canadian philosopher Charles Taylor, and since there are some ethical similarities between the *Gita*'s philosophy and Kant's philosophy, adding an appendix to the thesis on their ethical affinities was much more demanding. So, I added a fresh chapter to the thesis titled 'Nishkama Karma and the Categorical Imperative: A Philosophical Reflection on the Bhagavad-Gita'.[4] If you allow me, I would like to briefly highlight two close similarities for the readers. Firstly, the doer or agency in both the *Gita* and Kant substantively has a moral character with the knowledge of good and bad, but due to internal and external factors, the agency fails to make the correct moral decisions. Secondly, both the *Gita* and Kant are non-consequentialists as they both speak about duty for duty's sake or *karma for karma's sake*.

The Eastern wisdom of ancient India

In one article, you compare Kant's epistemology to the work of Indian philosopher Jiddu Krishnamurti. Are their concepts similar in any way?

I must say that as far as I know this was the first paper of its kind as I have not seen or read any other research paper on Kant and Krishnamurti till now.[5] To your specific question about the conceptual similarities in their philosophies, I would say that their ways of thinking are quite different and so are their philosophical thoughts. For example, Kant speaks of the conditioned (human) mind which has twelve pure concepts as its own categories of understanding, *apriorily* applicable to all objects of possible cognition. That means, knowledge is impossible if these concepts are not applied by the mind. Krishnamurti, in an epistemological contrast to Kant, speaks of the unconditioned mind which gets knowledge of truth and reality directly. He calls it intuitive knowledge or highest intelligence, which can happen 'when the mind is unconditioned or free from all concepts and sensuous representations'.[6] For him, the conditioned mind 'keeps us away from the truth and reality.' However, two similarities in their philosophical positions can be mentioned: a) They both believe that the human mind is rational and can reach the highest point of intellect, and b) some mental representations involve s*pontaneity*, particularly in case of *intellectual* intuition.

You have also written about the pessimist philosopher Arthur Schopenhauer's reading of Upanishadic wisdom. Few Westerners had studied Hinduism in his day. Was Schopenhauer's reading well-informed?

This is an interesting question. Let me respond to your question with reference to my comments on this in an earlier paper.[7] See, Schopenhauer was a German by birth but was very much Indian by thinking. This must have been the sole reason, I believe, that he preferred the Indian idealism of the Upaniṣads' monistic philosophy over German idealism. And since the Upaniṣads don't talk of pessimism, I find it very difficult to call Schopenhauer a pessimist philosopher. Maybe that is a German way of understanding him. Nonetheless, you are right when you say that few Westerners also studied Hinduism in his day. For example, German Indologists like Gottfried Herder (1744–1803), Friedrich von Schlegel (1772–1829), Heinrich Heine (1797–1856), Max Müller (1823–1900) and a few others who were contemporary to Schopenhauer did study Indian Sanskrit texts including the Upaniṣads. But I am not sure, as I have no textual proof, of whether they were well-informed about Schopenhauer's reading of Hinduism. I can only assume with reasons that it is quite unlikely that Schopenhauer's life and works were unexplored by his contemporaries and successors.

Has Schopenhauer cut through in *Indian* thought in light of the attention he paid to its key texts? Is he read, quoted, debated by Indian philosophers?

Yes, Schopenhauer has been one of the many German philosophers who has the most cut through with Indian scholars, but as App indicates, possibly his 'encounter with Indian thought is a historical sequence of events'.[8] However, it is true that Schopenhauer is a figure who is widely known, read, quoted, and debated by Indian philosophers. In fact, Schopenhauer's love for Indian wisdom fascinates Indian researchers, particularly those who work on the Indo-German relationship or the East-West connection and the vital role played by the shared intellectual histories of the two countries. Likewise, it would not be an exaggeration to say that philosopher Schopenhauer's intellectual passion for Indian philosophy ignited many German and other European minds to study Indian philosophical texts. And now an enthusiastic trend to study Indian philosophy and the Sanskrit language is rapidly growing in Germany.

You have written in defence of vegetarianism. What moral duties do we have towards animals and do you think some animals have a moral sense?

The Eastern wisdom of ancient India

You have asked a very pertinent question. Since I am known to be frank and loud in speaking my mind on animal issues, I always argue that vegetarianism is one of the issues which is directly linked with our moral duties and behaviour towards animals. What duties, you ask? Don't we know that life *in itself* and in all forms is valuable, and that this is what determines the value of human life? So, we humans have no right to kill animals, if animals don't accept such a human *right to kill* and give us their consent. And I am not convinced by the argument that animals have no moral sense. Some of them do have a moral sense, even better than that of humans. Don't you think that unharmful animals are better than harmful humans? I think we should have fair reasons, though I know many of us don't have, to support the claim that animal killing that serves the purpose of non-vegetarianism is justified. In fact, it is very irritating to argue with those who project animals as inferior beings and defend their sickness to human superiority. I hope you don't get me wrong. Even if you do, I must submit a loud claim that we all have categorial duties towards animals, for example not to harm their lives (that means not to kill them, no matter whatever compelling reasons one has), to provide them with a favourable ecosystem, and to stop encroaching on them and exploiting their life.

The ancient Greek philosopher Pythagoras is said to have taught vegetarianism, which some even think he picked up sojourning in India. How much stock do you put in the theory of early Greek-Indian exchanges?

I am happy that you have mentioned Pythagoras, who is believed to have been greatly influenced by ancient cardinal virtues like *ahiṃsā* (nonviolence) and vegetarianism. But if you ask me to prove this belief by producing a textual reference, I would say I have a very little stock to put in the theory of early Greek-Indian exchanges. For instance, I can cite the Roman philosopher Lucius Apuleius (124-170 AD) and the Irish William Drummond (*The Rights of Animals*, 1838) who were of the opinion that Pythagoras visited India and learnt a lot from this land.[9] That precisely answers your question. However, even if there is no proof for whether or not Pythagoras picked up the idea of vegetarianism from India, I do believe that being a vegetarian is the best way to vitalise the human-animal relationship from the animal perspective, because animals are a human obligation, not a human prey.

There's growing interest in non-Western philosophy in Western universities. What are some of the debates in contemporary philosophy in which you'd like to see more comparative engagement with Indian and Hindu thought?

This is true that non-Western philosophy is now in greater demand among the students at Western universities, also among the students at Eastern universities of Japan, Korea, Thailand, and several others. The reason that I can see is that the world has now realised that the Eastern wisdom of classical, ancient India has much more to enhance their thinking, their knowledge and their worldviews. This is why in my recent interviews published by the American Philosophical Association I suggested that Indian philosophy, be it Hinduism or Buddhism or Jainism, must be taught at Western universities.[10] But as far as your specific question is concerned, I would say that I would like to see more comparative engagement with Indian and Hindu thought on the issues of the origin and function of language, cognitive patterns of intuitive knowledge, mystical orientation, divinisation of the environment, Vedic mathematics, metaphysics of rituals, metaphysics of silence, and Hindu cosmology, *etc.* if I am to list them.

Who is the one Indian thinker you wish every undergraduate philosophy student outside India knew and why?

Although every Indian philosopher and founders of various philosophical schools, particularly of the classical period, should be known and read by the students of philosophy, if you are asking me to pick one philosopher then I would say that it is Ādi Śaṅkarācārya, who had a very short span of life but his original Sanskrit writings and commentaries on the classical Hindu texts have treasured most of the ancient Indian wisdom. So, I would wish for students outside India to read Ādi Śaṅkarācārya and his philosophy, as I believe he presents deeper philosophical insights about life and the world than other philosophers do.

Conversely, which non-Indian thinkers do you think should be more widely read in the Indian academy and in philosophy schools in particular?

I will name Immanuel Kant (1724-1804), the 18th century German philosopher whose profound philosophical thinking has revolutionised the human quest and efforts for knowledge and truth. His theories offer deeper cognitive reflections to a rational mind. So, I think Kant should be more widely read in the Indian academy, particularly in philosophy schools.

Notes

1 Krishna Mani Pathak (ed.), *Quietism, Agnosticism and Mysticism: Mapping the Philosophical Discourse of the East and the West* (Singapore: Springer, 2021).
2 Pathak, *Quietism, Agnosticism and Mysticism*, 229-248.
3 Pathak, *Quietism, Agnosticism and Mysticism*, 238-243.
4 This appendix was later published in the *International Journal of Applied Ethics*, Vol. 2 (2013-14), 119-140.
5 Pathak, 'Intuition as a Blend of Cognition and Consciousness: An Examination in the Philosophies of Kant and Krishnamurti', in Steve Palmquist (ed.), *Kant on Intuition: Western and Asian Perspectives on Transcendental Idealism* (New York: Routledge, 2018), 200-215.
6 Pathak, 'Intuition as a Blend of Cognition and Consciousness', 208.
7 Pathak, 'The Quintessence of the Upanishadic Wisdom and the Solace of Schopenhauer's Life', in Arati Barua (ed.), *Schopenhauer on Self, World, and Morality: Vedantic and Non-Vedantic Perspectives* (Singapore: Springer, 2017), 59-68.
8 Urs App, 'Schopenhauer's Initial Encounter with Indian Thought', in *Schopenhauer Jahrbuch*, Vol. 87 (2006), 35-76.
9 See also Rod Preece, *Sins of the Flesh: A History of Ethical Vegetarian Thought* (Vancouver: UBC, 2008).

10 The interview was published in two parts. The first part was published on 5 September 2022 and the second was published on 3 October 2022. See 'Reports from Abroad: Dr. Krishna Mani Pathak', *Blog of the American Philosophical Association*, available at: <https://blog.apaonline.org/?s=krishna+pathak>.

STORIES

The first white men*

Georges Baudoux†

TRANSLATED BY *Daryl Morini*‡

I
'That old Tchiao' (1919)

Tchiao is a really old Kanak from the village of Bouaganda, right near the big tribe in Gomen. You know the one, that little cluster of pointed huts lying hidden in a bouquet of dark trees and tall pine trees, straight as spears. The little hamlet is seen from afar. It's as isolated as an island in the grassy, blond foothills that prop up the great peak at Kaala. It's plopped there at the foot of a wall of slender stones jutting up like needles, which always seems about to collapse onto, and flatten, the village. But it stays there, and the Kanaks aren't scared; moreover, the sorcerers, they who know much, said there was nothing to fear from it. And when it was said by sorcerers, that was that.

---

* These are the first known complete English translations of *Ce vieux Tchiao* ('That old Tchiao', 1919) and *L'Épouvante* ('A horror story', 1939). These stories were republished in the collection: Georges Baudoux, *Légendes Canaques II: Ils Avaient vu des Hommes Blancs* (Paris: Nouvelles Éditions Latines, 1952). This work is in the public domain.

† Georges Baudoux (1870-1949), a.k.a. Thiosse, was the first New Caledonian writer. He worked as a cobalt and nickel miner on the main island's northwest, where he collected oral history. He lived in Nouméa, Koumac, Koné.

‡ Daryl Morini is the editor of *Synkrētic* and a researcher and translator of Russian philosophy. He holds a PhD in International Relations from the University of Queensland. He is based in Canberra, Australia.

The first white men

It's pretty when you're there, in Bouaganda. Far, far off in the distance you can see the sea and a white line made of frothing waves colliding against big reefs. One sees Devert island, where turtles and birds lay their eggs, and the Bay of Téoudié, where many fish dance their *pilou*.[1] And below, the Gomen plains, which stretch out their mats of every green and yellow hue beneath the sun. One constantly hears the water falling from Kaala mountain, thundering in the valleys deep.

Tchiao is so old a Kanak that he has no age, he's far too old for it. He walks as if his back had snapped in half, and he's thin, so thin. He's made of bones and nerves stretched as tight as rope made of *taoura*;[2] he's just a living skeleton covered in black skin, dried and cracked, all crease and wrinkle. His shaven skull gleams like a dry coconut, he's lost all but a few hairs scattered about his head, in his ears too. His beard, clumpy and yellow, is of a kind rarely seen. The sun dazzles his bleary eyes, so he shuts them. To walk, he leans with both hands on a long stick. Being a bit fussy, as Tchiao is, he doesn't want to talk to anyone and always mutters to himself.

But Tchiao has a story. He saw many things and knew the time of the heroes, but his memories get all scrambled, so when he tells them he makes mistakes. He no longer knows. When the first white men, albinos from another island, came to Gomen, he was there, Tchiao was, in all his adult power and his martial glory. He didn't slay them, these first white men; he knew the delicate taste of human meat, which he often ate.[3] But now, when asked if he ate white man,[4] he denies it and clicks his old red tongue which is ever wiggling at the back of his always half-opened mouth.

When he was young, Tchiao was a man open to progress.[5] He knew, thanks to the Pouébo Kanaks, that the whites would bring many useful things, and that killing them was unwise. In exchange for yams and *ouaré*,[6] the white men offered pickaxes to replace the poles used to till the soil. As well as iron axes that were better for cutting serpentine rock and that never chipped.[7] He had seen the whites come to cut sandalwood with their quick axes; he, Tchiao, had been overawed. To gain one, he had had to give the white men two of his own stone axes which the ancestors had bequeathed him.

Synkrētic

He had tasted, too, the white man's yams, which tasted nicer than Kanak yams. They were more subtle and didn't stick to the roof of your mouth. But the whites always sliced their yams and only gave away the offcuts. But he, Tchiao, wanted a whole one to himself.

One day, Tchiao saw the white man's great *pirogues*,[8] with its two masts and many sails. The *pirogues* cast anchor in Youanga Bay. Tchiao grabbed two coconut-palm baskets, filled them with yams, and placed them on the back of his wife, who meekly followed.

He came to the seashore, opposite the ship, and sat on the beach, waiting until the white men wished to come ashore.

Kanak *pirogues* lay in the creeks and mangroves, one of which he could have taken to board, but this would have been ill-advised. If he'd gotten onto the ship, the whites would have killed him for meat. This was obvious.

Being obdurate and patient like his people, he waited the whole day for a tender boat to approach the shore. To distract himself, he fished for crabs and fish. At night, when the sun sank in the sea, he camped out a little further with his wife, both well concealed, so the whites wouldn't kill them in their sleep.

The next day, a tender peeled away from the schooner and came ashore. Tchiao went in, the water up to his thighs, the better to show himself while his wife fled, squatting low like a sultana bird,[9] to hole up in the long grass.

The closer the tender came, the more steps back Tchiao took to stay a healthy distance away from the white men. These white men were strong out here, on the waves and ashore, so one had to be cautious. And while there were many whites, he, Tchiao, was by himself. If they attacked him, he could only rely on his legs to get away.

He parlayed with the white men who came ashore, making signs, always at a distance, which was enough to make himself understood. Tchiao dropped on the sand his two baskets full of yams, and the white men lobbed one his way that he caught mid-flight. With the deal done, Tchiao left to meet his wife, who was waiting for him on the ground, curled up in the straw.

Tchiao's life changed from this day on, acquiring a quite mysterious aura in other Kanaks' eyes. He'd leave early with the morning sun, without saying where, and would never bring anything back.

At times, he'd climb a peak, always the same one, carrying a basket containing his own assortment of herbs. From the ground, he'd be seen gesticulating in ways foreign to all the Kanaks: he was engaging in devilry and magic. But this made no sense, for Tchiao wasn't a sorcerer, he wasn't, but he was becoming one. All Kanaks, including women and children,[10] started to fear him.

It was worrying enough that the sorcerers met as a Council, in which they decided that Tchiao's designs had to be investigated. What kind of calamities was he calling upon the tribe? What kind of unknown devil[11] did he speak to? Whose death was he plotting? To stave off his evil spells, perhaps it was time that Tchiao be killed.

All the tribe's sorcerers watched him, taking note of his coming and going, and of his gestures. They also studied the herbs Tchiao was using. He was always seen leaving his bouquet of herbs behind on the cliff, and latching onto a perch that was jammed in the earth. Tchiao had noticed he was being watched, so he would vary his departure times, changing the paths he took, resorting to trickery. Since Tchiao had become a special kind of sorcerer, the sorcerers grew scared of him and wavered in their murderous intent. Once he had been killed, he'd come back all horrible at night, when it was dark.

This witchcraft of his, which they were getting used to, had gone on for a few moons when a chance event helped the actual sorcerers discover the curses that dreaded Tchiao was practising.

He was in a little clearing of the forest, running in circles between a dozen yam poles planted upright; he held the herbs in his hands, dangling them about; at times he fell on all fours, and he brought his lips close to the soil, from where he spoke to it. Tchiao wanted to spoil the yam harvest, there was no longer any doubt about it.

The next day, the great Chief of Gomen sent his guards to detain the evil Tchiao. The great Council of sorcerers was gathered when he arrived. The executioner hung around, awaiting orders.

The Chief accused Tchiao of having cast a spell on the yams, to kill off all the tribe's yams.

Tchiao defended himself bravely: 'No! That's not true. Those are the white man's yams that I planted, since here only I can make them grow. I call the rain to come. I ask the dead who know how to make yams grow[12] to help me grow the white man's yam at night.'

His defence speech was strong, but it was time for the evidence. The whole august Counsel, executioners in their wake, travelled over to the forest clearing. Tchiao pointed out the base of a perch, which was searched, and bits of peelings from the white man's yams were found.

Tchiao had planted a whole bread, but thankfully for him there was some crust left over. The other perches had been planted as deception measures.

In a secret gathering, the Council of sorcerers came to the following conclusion: 'The white man's yams grow only in the white man's soil; they can't grow in the black man's soil.'

But now, Tchiao is old, oh so old, and young Kanaks who work for white men, who wear shorts and drink rum,[13] only mock him, saying: 'Ah, that old Tchiao is so mad. He, old Tchiao, wanted to make the white Kanak's[14] yams grow so the whole tribe could have a big feast.[15] He failed because the other Kanaks did him in.' Intuitively, old man Tchiao knows something has gone awry in nature's course.

And since he's a bit hard of hearing, when he sees white men or Kanaks look at him smiling, he still believes they're talking about the bread. And old Tchiao pouts his lower lip and clicks his tongue, and he walks off leaning on his walking stick, a symbol of the fading past.

II
'A horror story' (1939)

Come nightfall, the tropical sky brimming with starry millions hums in imposing silence. Abolishing all sense of perspective, a dark mass of mountains rises sharply, as does the wall that holds the sea at bay.[16] Near the coast, confused among trees, a brown boat's upturned image is reflected deep in the sea. Along its shore, against which waves crash gently, a little fire is lit. The trembling flames light up the underside of branches, move the shadows, and fashion a high ceiling out of the canopies.

Next to the intimate fire, a microcosmic speck in the vast outer world, two people talk gravely about a physiological question which a Kanak legend linked to this place has raised.

During their conversation, the coconut tree's long and bendy fronds rattle from the wind's passing caress. High up in the valley, a waterfall overwhelms the silence by crashing, droning, and whispering through the rocks. It tends to stop, then start again. The waterfall, its pitch modulated by the changing breeze, at times echoes the deep, murmuring voices of the spirits and ghosts that lurk in the gullies. Yes, this waterfall does speak, repeating the cryptic words of the ancestors, who never die.

Though now overrun by weeds whose roots cover every inch, one may find many horticultural ridges, round foundations for huts, and the stones of fireplaces in this area, signs of a time when a major Kanak town existed in this pleasant bay.

This tribe of fishermen who lacked for nothing, what became of them? Nobody knows. Nobody can say. Facing the threat of white men on great *pirogues* that could shoot lightning, and feeling squeezed between sea and mountain, they had had to scatter, had to join other tribes that had more free space, that were more determined to be independent.

The ancestral stories alone had escaped oblivion to remain tied to the missing tribe's land. In the silence of the night, when contented nature is most garrulous, these stories re-awaken a whole past that has been asleep for centuries.

The attractive Tili, who is near the fire, her midriff bare, with a fringe belt around her hips, has a good posture, her skin cast a brassy red colour, with a well-proportioned body.

Her hair is styled in a big, undulating ball that covers her eyes and hangs on her shoulders. She looks Polynesian but is said to be the daughter of a sandalwood trader, one of those colonial settlers who, once upon a time, had dreamed up the euphemism "breaking wood"[17] and left behind living proof of this work.

Although raised in a Kanak tribe, Tili possesses mental faculties greatly above those of ordinary tribeswomen; at any rate, the young white man who befriended her is under this illusion, which makes his life better.

In the daytime, in broad daylight, Tili's life is all smiles. She finds joy in all things and in nothing at all. She sees it in the alarmed bird fluttering after an insect. In the fish which leaps high in the air and lands on the water with a slap. In the little crab that flees with its pincers all frenzied, knitting its legs about, and sinks into its hole. These are the memorable events that only entertain her, comparing them as she does to human gestures.

Nature gives her all the fineries she desires, and which she picks up in passing, on a whim. She makes a scarf out of a blossoming vine. Should a scared bird's sudden flight leave a feather on the wind, she seizes it forthwith, sliding it behind her ear. She studs her hair with the scarlet flowers that she comes across. She wraps a small seashell that she finds around her wrist with plant fibres. This peace is not troubled by the thought that she may have to find something to eat. When the time comes, she knows nature will provide.

But at night, everything changes. When darkness warps the shape of all things and twists their outlines, making burnt niaouli trees[18] look like ghosts standing still, and when slumberous nature's whispers impress the mournful incantations of distant voices on one's mind, Tili falls prey to the superstitions she inherited from her Melanesian ancestors, she loses her touching carelessness, the slightest unexplained noise disturbs her, and Tili feels very small.

The young European who became Tili's partner after the last *pilou* tries his hardest to convince her that all these stories about revenants, ghosts, and devils, nefarious to varying degrees, are the product of the Kanaks' anxious imaginations, and that these fables are of no consequences. And this conversation is still going.

Tili objects: 'Of course you'd say that! Because you don't know, you've never seen it. But the old Kanaks from long ago, they saw, and they knew.'

'They were hallucinating, the elders, they saw devils everywhere. The elders before that, the ancestors, knew even less than today's elders.'

Tili: 'You don't need the elders to know. Listen to the waterfall up there, at the end of the valley. Hear that? It's not the water talking. Water can't talk. When the voices stop and come back very faintly, that's the devils talking about things from long ago.'

'What do they look like, the mean devils that are always chattering? We never see them.'

'Of course, we never see them. In the daytime they press into the forests of the mountain, but at night they come out and walk around, they observe how men and women live. If someone walks towards them, they hide in the bushes and the rocks. Although you don't see them, they are there; you can hear leaves rustling. Often, they dive deep into the water, where they talk to eels. That's when you can no longer hear them.'

'And what can the devils possibly tell eels that is of any interest to them?'

'That, I can't say. That's a Kanak thing. White people wouldn't understand.'

'You don't want to say because you have no idea. You're just kidding around. If you knew it, you'd tell me at once.'

'No. The devils in waterfalls, that's taboo. I can tell you about the other devils.'

'Okay, then tell me a story about devils, one that everyone can be told. Go on, tell me!'

With an air of conviction, Tili began: 'You know that from Paagoumène Point,[19] the one you can see over there, you can hear devils do *pilou* dances in the mountain's caves at night. As soon as it's dark, the Kanaks no longer approach from this side. They stop before crossing the mountain pass, using the little path dug into the serpentine rock that goes down from Paagoumène Bay to Ohlande Bay. To throw off the devils, the Kanaks light fires along the seashore, then they sleep there, in the sand, till daybreak. If the Kanaks walked that path at night, when it's dark, the dead would come to kill them.'

Just as Tili spoke of the dangers that awaited the Kanaks at night, the dry branch of a nearby tree broke and, with a long *cr-a-a-ck*, fell to the earth with a heavy thud, unleashing a roaring sound that awoke the valleys' echoes.

Tili leapt to her feet at once and, with her eyes fixed on the source of the noise in the dark, she stood ready to leap into the water to make for the boat that might save her.

Her boyfriend gestured to stop her: 'Come on! Please don't. There's nothing to fear. That rotten branch was pulled down by its own weight. It had to fall sometime. Take a seat here. It's over. What are you afraid of?'

Still surveying the gloom from whence threats can emerge, Tili expressed her desire to go elsewhere immediately.

'See, I told you so!' she said. 'That branch didn't break by itself. Someone had to give it a push. A mountain devil did it. I know it. He followed the creeks[20] to the sea. That's where he heard my voice. He was listening and understood that I was talking about the devils that bring death to men. So, he got mad and broke a big branch to tell me to get away, that he'd hurt me if I stayed here.'

'Oh, come on, Tili, stop being ridiculous. None of that's possible, as you know full well. Just sit here quietly and let's not talk of this broken branch again. We're fine here, we have fire. Surely you don't expect us to pack up right now to go camp elsewhere?'

Feeling threatened by a danger only she can comprehend, Tili doesn't give up hope of leaving. She stands up and, with knees drawn tight, says in protest: 'Of course you fear nothing, you want to stay here. But me, I'm scared. Me, if I sit on this ground, that's it, I'll die.'

'What are you talking about? Dying! That's a stretch. No one wants to hurt you. And I'm here.'

'Yes, you're here, but you know nothing. You'll see nothing. It'll be too late when you see.'

The first white men

'Now, that's better. At least explain yourself clearly. What danger are you facing? Tell me so I can protect you from it.'

With eyes still locked on the bush, across which shadows cast by the fire's flickering flames swayed, Tili decided to explain a few things: 'We've been here since morning. We walked around here, we picked up breadfruit.[21] You, you're happy. You swam in the waterfall's deep swimming holes, and I watched you doing it. But I didn't swim.'

'Well, you didn't swim because you didn't feel like it. But that's no reason to run off in the middle of the night.'

'I didn't swim because the elders made it taboo to do so way back. They knew things. They'd seen things. They placed the taboo. We have to listen to the elders.'

'They placed a taboo on what, exactly?'

Tili hesitates, ums and ahs, and finally decides to lift a portion of the veil. Men can swim in the waterfall, but women can't. It's taboo. Some evil eels are found in there. Those eels are the same colour as the rocks. They can't be seen.

'So, what do they do, these evil eels?'

'Ah! Well, there's no use saying it. You know full well.'

'Well, no. I know nothing. How am I meant to know, since you're not saying anything specific. You always talk a lot, but don't say much.'

Tili casts off the burden haunting her mind by sharing this secret: 'You know that eels slither. They force their way into women, where they bite them and make them die.'

'Right, now I understand. That's awful. But if you don't enter the water, then surely you have nothing to fear from these eels.'

'Of course I do! There's still plenty to fear. When devils order them to do so, the eels leave the water at night. They slither like snakes in the grass and, guided by scent, go to places where they'll find sleeping women to hurt.'

Because, after hearing this explained, it would have been in poor taste and most ungrateful to force the virtuous Tili to spend all night standing next to the fire, deathly afraid, they both rolled up their mats and left to sleep at the bottom of their rowboat, away from the coast and far from the famished eels. And that's it.

※

It would be idle to seek the genesis of this Kanak tale, which arose from unclear circumstances and was transformed into a supernatural tale under the influence of credulous imaginations and charismatic sorcerers. Let us only note that this drama's powerful sway extended over Ohlande Bay half a century ago,[22] and that, since then, an invasive civilisation with no respect for taboos had upturned the domain of ancient tradition.

So it came to be that Paagoumène Bay—where once, beneath the shadeful banyan trees, lay storied, decomposing skeletons, brightly glistening jaws, and brachycephalous skulls[23] caught between mossy stones and tangled vines—was now dominated by the opulent house of a certain *Monsieur le Directeur* of a mining site.[24] The ancestors' bones had been swept away.[25]

The narrow trail dug over centuries, the one which the Kanaks dared not cross by night, was now blocked off by corrugated iron buildings, in which the roar of engines and of anvils ringing under hammer blows could be heard. No, these are no longer the sounds of the past.

Meanwhile, on the other side beyond the mountain pass, in the small plain to which ghosts are exiled at night and which dampens the noise from the waves that crash against the reefs to the rhythm of an underground *pilou* dance, civilised men had lined up their graveyard's burial mounds in even rows. The mantra of superior races is always this: 'Move, you're in my place!'[26]

In the spot called Paagougne, a little further in Ohlande Bay, near a beach whose shore is lined with seaweed and under coconut trees swaying in the wind, right in front of the waterfall haunted by misogynistic eels, a rural French settler farms pigs like some latter-day Eumaeus.[27] The world has ended.

Faced with these desecrations, there is no doubt that all the Kanak devils, little dwarves,[28] mysterious eels, and *toguis*[29] must have

The first white men

holed themselves up in caves to give way to Greek hydras,[30] old satyrs,[31] gnomes, and wood goblins[32]—creatures which, by virtue of becoming official mythological entities, have now gained the right to live anywhere they like, including in the souls of the civilised.

Notes

I
'That old Tchiao' (1919)

1 P. 9: A *pilou* (or *pilou-pilou*), from the Nyelâyu language's *pilu* meaning 'to dance', is a traditional Kanak ceremony. It tended to involve group dancing by night in a circular motion around a pole for hours.

2 P. 36: *Taoura*: a word, likely borrowed from Tahitian, for a thin rope made from plant fibres. *Te Reo*, Vol. 1-7 (1958): 5.

3 P. 37: Karin Speedy, a translator of and authority on Georges Baudoux, notes that 'when we examine Boudoux's stories today, we cannot help but notice when,' as here, 'he surrenders to the sensationalism of the colonial genre. Violent scenes of savagery and cannibalism, for instance, serve to justify the colonial project,' using tropes of the Kanaks as animals, children, primitives, brutal, superstitious, at the bottom of civilisation's ladder, etc. 'Baudoux's *Légendes Canaques* are steeped in racist discourses,' as Speedy writes. But she notes that their paradoxical nature makes them relevant reading today. There is a dualism in his works, a surprisingly critical depiction of colonisation's 'metaphoric cannibalism' of Kanak society. 'Here we have the sublime ambiguity of Baudoux—for, if the black world is savage, frightening and brutal the "civilised" white world is no less cruel and inhuman.' See Karin Speedy, 'Critical Introduction, Georges Baudoux, *Jean M'Baraï, the Trepang Fisherman* (Sydney: UTS ePRESS, 2007), 26, 40.

4 P. 37: 'if he ate white man' (*s'il a caïcayé du tayo blanc*) contains two Kanak pidgin words now absorbed into New Caledonian French. *Caïcayer* is a francised verb of the Pidgin (*kakae* in Bislama) loan word *caïcaï*, 'to eat', 'meal', 'feast'. *Tayo* is a Polynesian word which, instead of 'friend', means 'Kanak man' locally. Speedy, in *Jean M'Baraï*, 23.

5 P. 37: See note 3 for context on the depiction of Tchiao as 'a man open to progress' (*l'esprit ouvert au progrès*).

6 P. 37: *Ouaré* is the lesser yam (*Dioscorea esculenta*). Some suggest it was a sweet, served with sugar cane and bananas.

7 P. 37: 'Iron axes' (*tamioc en fer*): A tamioc, which may be derived from 'tomahawk', is a stone hatchet and weapon.

Synkrētic

8   P. 9: *Pirogue* is the French word for Kanak sailboats made from timber canoes, stabilised either using an outrigger or in some cases a second hull connected by a deck, and with one or two triangle-shaped sails like the modern sloop.

9   P. 39: The sultana bird (*poule sultane*) is the western swampen (*Porphyrio porphyrio*), a chicken-sized wetland bird.

10 P. 40: Children (*pikinini*) is a term for 'Kanak children', as Baudoux explains in a footnote.

11 P. 40: Devils (*togui*) is a term for 'devils and evil spirits', as Baudoux explains in a footnote.

12 P. 42: In Melanesia, garden magic rituals, chants, spells are conducted to protect a yam harvest and help it grow.

13 P. 43: 'drink rum' (*boivent du tafia*) is a reference to a local term for rum, *tafia*, used in other French colonies. The historian Frédéric Angleviel writes that '*tafia* spread to the mainland with the establishment of the penal colony,' and that 'the sale of alcohol to Melanesians was banned,' as well as to prisoners as a form of punishment. See Frédéric Angleviel (ed.), *Histoire de la Nouvelle-Calédonie: Nouvelles approches, nouveaux objets* (Paris: Harmattan, 2005), 34.

14 P. 43: 'the white Kanak' (*le tayo blanc*), a play on the fact that *tayo* refers to a Kanak man. See note 4.

15 P. 43: 'a big feast' (*un grand caï-caï*). See note 4.

II
'A horror story' (1939)

16 P. 171: In the context of the nightfall that, the narrator tells us, warps an object's perspective, 'the wall that holds the sea at bay' (*une muraille contenant la mer*) likely refers to the outer reef on the horizon.

17 P. 173: Some attribute to Kanak creole the now-defunct euphemism 'breaking wood' (*casser bois*) for coitus, but its use was also recorded on Vanuatu's Ambrym Island. This suggests Baudoux was right that European traders at least spread this term. See Henri le Chartier, *La Nouvelle-Calédonie et les Nouvelles-Hébrides* (Paris, Jouvet et cie, 1885), 243.

18 P. 174: The paperbark or tea tree (*Melaleuca quinquenervia*), known locally as niaouli (from the Bélep language *yauli*), is endogenous to New Caledonia as well as to eastern Australia. It is omnipresent on the mainland's west coast.

19 P. 177: Baudoux uses the outdated spelling Pagoumène, modernised in this version. Some sources spell the original local Kanak name as *Phwaaxuman*.

20 P. 178: 'Creek' (*le creek*) has been absorbed into New Caledonia French, probably from Australian English.

21 P. 179: 'Breadfruit' (*mayorés*) or *Artocarpus altilis* is an endogenous tree whose floury-textured fruit tastes sweet.

22 P. 180: 'half a century ago' implies that the story is set around 1889 and that the storyteller is telling it in 1939.

23 P. 182: 'brachycephalous' (lit. 'short-skulled') refers to the then-prevalent belief that Kanak heads were so shaped. Though it originated in medicine, where it is still used, the term's now-discredited use in anthropology in late 19th and early 20th century Europe was associated with the widespread racist, anti-Semitic, social Darwinist ideas of the time. The French eugenicist Georges Vacher de Lapouge, whose ideas influenced Hitler, theorised that the *Homo Alpinis* race was small, dark, brachycephalous, and lazy. The *Homo Europeaus* or Aryan race was superior, he wrote, because its members were tall, blond, energetic, intelligent, war-like, long-skulled (dolichocephalous), and rode bicycles. Nietzsche endorsed the idea that the 'inferior race' had 'brachycephalous features'. But other anthropologists at the time rejected Lapouge's classification, seeing brachycephalous heads as the true mark of superiority. Stuart K. Hayashi, *Hunting Down Social Darwinism: Will This Canard Go Extinct?* (Lanham, Maryland: Lexington Books, 2015), 138; Mike Hawkins, 'Social Darwinism and Race', in *A Companion to Nineteenth-Century Europe, 1789-1914*, ed. Stefan Berger (Main Street, Madden: Blackwell Publishing, 2006), 231; Nietzsche, cited in Georges Chatterton-Hill, *The Philosophy of Nietzsche: An Exposition and an Appreciation* (New York: Haskell, 1971 [1914]), 197; Mike Hawkins, *Social Darwinism in European and American Thought, 1860-1945* (Cambridge: Cambridge University Press, 1997), 193 fn. 35, 194.

24 P. 182: *Monsieur le Directeur*, the polite French form of address for a director, refers to the manager of the mine in the area in Paagoumène Bay in the late 1930s. The bay was then part of the large chromium mine based in Tiébaghi, the largest in the world in 1941, at one time owned by BHP. It ceased operations in 1990. The bay in which the story is set was used to load the ships bound for Marseille and New York and was likely, as Baudoux suggests, the location of the executive director's home, at the time a *Monsieur le Directeur Adminsitratif* A. Magnin. See 'La Tiébaghi à Paagoumène (Nouvelle-Calédonie): chrome', in *Entreprises Coloniales*, 21 January 2019, available at: < https://entreprises-coloniales.fr/pacifique/Tiebaghi_chrome.pdf>.

25 P. 182: At the time of writing, the land around Ohland Bay and Paagoumène Bay remains either under a mining cadastre that extends around the old Tiébaghi mining site or privately owned land. No tribe is officially registered in the area. This west coast region saw some of the most ferocious dispossessions of Kanak land in New Caledonia's history. In 1900, the Gomen chief committed suicide after his entire tribal domain was given to a settler. Some sources suggest that this event impacted Kanaks in Paagoumène as well. Jean Guiart, 'Naissance et avortement d'un messianisme', in *Archives de Sciences Sociales des Religions*, Issue 7 (January-June 1959): 7.

26 P. 182: 'Move, you're in my place!' (*Ôte-toi de là que je m'y mette*) is a French expression with a meaning related to the English 'possession is nine-tenths of the law', but with a sarcastic bite that is critical of this attitude.

27 P. 182: Eumaeus is a Greek mythological figure, swineherd, and friend to Odysseus in *The Odyssey*.

Synkrētic

28. P. 183: 'little dwarves' (*kââ-goumè*), which Baudoux doesn't define, appears to be the local term for the mystical, often malevolent dwarves of Kanak mythology, which are typically feared and called *nains* or *lutins* in French. In the Nêlêmwa-Nixumwak language, *kha-xuxum* means 'all tiny, like a dwarf' and *khaa-yu* means 'all small'. See Isabelle Bril and Soop Dahot, *Dictionnaire nêlêmwa-nixumwak-français-anglais* (Leuven: Peeters, 2000), 216.

29. P. 183: Some oral history supports Baudoux's attribution of Kanak mythical-religious significance to this location. A story narrated by François Pumali in the nearby village of Pagou (*Néyamwa*) on 25 September 1977 explains that, upon death, the Kanak soul enters the underworld at the same beach of Paagoumène (*Phwaaxuman*). It is there that the soul enters a cave occupied by a devil (or *togui*), down which it will travel to join the dead. See Maurice Coyaud and Denise Bernot, *Littérature orale: Birmanie, Corée, Japon, Mongolie, Nouvelle-Calédonie* (Paris : SELAF, 1979), 36.

30. P. 183: The *Hydra* is the Greek mythological serpent guarding the underworld, which Hercules kills in his labours.

31. P. 183: Translated as 'old satyrs' (*aux silures*), Baudoux is referring to Greek mythological creatures associated with Silenus, friend and tutor to the wine god Dionysus. *Sileni* were satyr-like creatures with horse's tails rather than goat's legs, and are sometimes synonyms for old satyrs. Greek art portrayed *sileni* as often lustful, usually drunk older men.

32. P. 183: 'wood goblin' (*sylvains*) are European mythical goblins or elves. In one account, they protect hazelnuts from naughty boys. Their name is derived from *Silvanus*, Roman god of the woods, from the Latin *silva* for 'forest'. Sylvans were thought to exist well into the Middle Ages. Thomas Aquinas mentions them in his *Summa Theologica* and appears to accept their existence, assimilating them to a group of demons that persecute women.

NOTES

On comparative philosophy

*Noel S. Pariñas**

Comparative philosophy is one of the emerging fields in philosophy in the Philippines nowadays not only in terms of scholars' preference but also because it has been included as one of the major courses by the Commission on Higher Education in the philosophy curriculum. What is comparative philosophy? This itself is a philosophical question, a difficult one, which causes much excitement and disagreement within the academy and beyond.

Comparative philosophy is an approach that allows us to look at philosophy in a different light. The area of study, however, needs clarification of the underlying assumption as to whether comparative philosophy should be treated as a systematic approach where philosophies are compared on the one hand, or using philosophy as a method to compare on the other hand. Questions like: 'How did the Western philosophers ask questions compared to the Eastern philosophers?', 'How are the questions raised by the Western philosophers different from the questions raised by the Eastern philosophers?', and 'Is there really a point in comparing apples and oranges?' presuppose metatheoretical assumptions that are helpful in laying down the foundations and setting the direction of a comparative philosophical inquiry. This is a relatively new area of study

---

* Noel S. Pariñas is an Assistant Professor of Philosophy at the University of the Philippines. He holds a PhD from Benguet State University and a JD from the University of Baguio. He sojourns in Baguio City, Philippines.

for the Western mainstream philosophers and even for Western-oriented philosophy scholars across the globe.

When we consider comparative philosophy as a systematic approach in which philosophies are compared, we simply compare philosophies beyond national colours. Claiming a comparison between Eastern and Western philosophies is problematic because philosophy is fundamentally Western. Obviously, German thoughts and Filipino thoughts are structurally different so that there is really no point in comparing apples and oranges. If the attempt is to appraise the common ground or similarities, then comparison must be focused on particular philosophies. For example, we compare Paulo Freire's notion of the 'new man' with that of Rajneesh Osho rather than comparing 'Brazilian philosophy' and 'Indian philosophy', because Freire's philosophy is not Brazilian philosophy and Osho's philosophy is not Indian philosophy. Why is this so? Because 'philosophy' is fundamentally Greek. It is the Greeks who described and defined such a system of thought.

There are philosophies in Germany as there are philosophies in the Philippines. But a philosophy in Germany or in the Philippines cannot be properly identified as German philosophy or Filipino philosophy respectively. There is no such thing as German philosophy or Filipino philosophy, only a German or a Filipino doing philosophy. Philosophy should be understood as an activity non-referent to nationality. It is not a citizen-based body of doctrine.

One could ask: If the western philosophers have problematised "being", what was the focus of the eastern thinkers' philosophical problematisation (if there is one)? Put another way: Are there eastern counterparts to the western cosmocentric/logocentric ancient period, theocentric mediæval period, anthropocentric modern period, and linguacentric contemporary period? The western philosophical epochs may serve as templates in the process of establishing a historical comparison of independent philosophical development.

In addition, we may as well contrast different systems of thought, namely *philosophy* (of Greek origin), *tetsugaku* (of Japanese origin), *zhexue* (of Chinese origin), *cheolhak* (of Korean origin), and

Synkrētic

batnayan (of Filipino origin) to determine the points of convergence without necessarily depending on Western light if possible. What is certain is that, first, these systems of thought are geared toward the formulation of meta-theories (theories of theories). For example, the political scientist studies politics to come up with political theory or a *theory of politics*, while the political philosopher studies political theory to come up with a *theory of the theory of politics*. Second, these systems of thought are scientific. They are scientific because they employ a systematic approach. By science, I herein refer to *speculative science* (where questions are more important than answers and in which the focus is on the growth of wisdom) and not *positive science* (where answers are more important than questions and in which the focus is on the growth of knowledge).

SUBMISSIONS

Australia and its place in the world continue to evolve. Now more than ever, we have to understand our region and our place in it. *Synkrētic* is an outlet for thought-provoking writing on philosophy, literature and cultures, from and about the Indo-Pacific. It aims to showcase the diverse traditions of thought, story-telling and expression which are woven into the living tapestry of this culturally, linguistically and politically complex region. We're looking above all for well-written and substantive pieces for publication in the following formats.

Essays	3000 - 6000 words
Stories	≤ 8000 words
Responses	800 - 1600 words
Translations	≤ 8000 words
Notes	300 - 3000 words

For details and guidelines:
synkretic.com

www.ingramcontent.com/pod-product-compliance
Lightning Source LLC
Chambersburg PA
CBHW020325010526
44107CB00054B/1986